Nativity

Nativity

*Reflections on Matthew's Story of
Jesus's Birth and Early Life*

Donald E. Burke

Donald E. Burke
Visit my website at www.donaldeburke.com

First Printing: Oct 2019

ISBN-13   978-1-0899161-3-0

Available through Amazon.com and other Amazon websites.

"...and you are to name him Jesus, for he will save his people from their sins..." (Matthew 1:21)

Table of Contents

Introduction

I have never been a big fan of Matthew's gospel. Sure, Matthew records Jesus's Sermon on the Mount (Matthew 5-7) but I have always found the story of Christmas in Matthew to be much less interesting than that told by Luke. Luke's story is filled with angels, animals, and shepherds...with glorious proclamations from the heavens in the night sky...and a Saviour who was born in a barn and placed in a manger. The birth of Jesus seems both so ordinary and so extraordinary at the same time. But in Matthew the actual birth of Jesus merits only passing mention. Matthew is more interested in the meaning of Jesus's origin and identity than in the details of his birth.

I have also preferred Luke because his portrayal of Jesus seems closer to my own inclinations. In Luke, Jesus associates with outcasts of many kinds. He takes his message to those who too often are left on the outside looking in. Luke's presentation of Jesus portrays him as one who has compassion on those he meets. Jesus's compassion is a hallmark of Luke.

On the other hand, sometimes Matthew is portrayed as a rigid, demanding gospel. Its emphasis on character and alternative values offends and sometimes can seem legalistic. The Sermon on the Mount for all of its virtues strikes many as being too idealistic, too demanding—even impossible to live up to. Jesus's exhortation to "Be perfect, therefore, as your heavenly Father is perfect," (Matthew 5:48) runs counter to the sentiment of our time when bumper sticker Christianity asserts, "I am not perfect, just forgiven."

So I am a little surprised that over the past several years, as I have studied the early chapters of Matthew and—for a separate project—the Lord's Prayer, my appreciation for Matthew's telling of the story of Jesus has grown so much. Matthew has a strong interest in the formation of the contrast community to which he addressed his Gospel. It is clear that Matthew understood Jesus to be calling together a new community—a renewed Israel—that would live out its identity in the kingdom of heaven. Matthew's Jesus emphasizes the "greater righteousness" to which the Church as a contrast community is called.

For Matthew, Jesus stands in the long tradition of Israel. His interpretation of Jesus is grounded in the Old Testament. Matthew frequently interprets the significance of events in the life of Jesus through the lens of the Old Testament prophets. For Matthew, Jesus stands as the key player in the long story of God's salvation-history. His coming marks the turning-point, the decisive moment in that history. With Jesus, the kingdom of heaven has come near!

Matthew's story of Jesus begins at the beginning. With a lengthy genealogy that traces Jesus's lineage back to Abraham, Matthew sets the stage for his presentation of Jesus. When examined carefully (and prayerfully), Matthew's Jesus emerges as a teacher, preacher, healer, servant and saviour. Jesus is all these things. But most fundamentally, Jesus is the Messiah (Christ), the Son of God who is also the son Abraham, the son of David, and the son of Joseph and Mary. This is the confession that shapes the early chapters of Matthew.

In the studies that follow we are going to examine the early chapters of Matthew's presentation of Jesus, prior to the public ministry of Jesus (Matthew 1:1–4:16). These chapters set the stage for the ministry of Jesus. They are foundational because here Matthew sets out his interpretation of the identity and mission of Jesus. They provide the lens through which to read the rest of Matthew.

It is possible to read these reflections through the Christian seasons of Advent, Christmas, and Epiphany. But they can speak to us at any time. So I invite you to follow Matthew's story of Jesus through these early chapters.

PART ONE: THE BIRTH OF JESUS

Chapter 1: Waiting and Hope

Matthew 1:1-17

Matthew situates the story of Jesus within the entire history of the Jewish people. In the opening verses of his Gospel, Matthew recounts — generation-by-generation — the lineage of Jesus from Abraham forward. By doing this he affirms that the story he is about to tell did not begin in Bethlehem during the reign of Herod the Great. From his perspective, the decisive events he is going to relate have been a long time coming to pass. Over the centuries Israel has been waiting...watching...longing for the coming of the kingdom of heaven and the one who would bring it.

WAITING IN ADVENT

The opening verses of Matthew are all about waiting and have a central place in the Christian season of Advent. Advent is a season of waiting and watching, a time of preparation and anticipation. It takes patience to get through Advent without rushing on to

Christmas and the rest of the story of Jesus. That's because waiting is not easy, especially for us in our time. We are accustomed to instant responses, instant meals, instant success, instant solutions to problems, instant messages, instant healing, and instant answers to prayer. We live in a world of megahertz, nanoseconds, and soundbites. Our lives are experienced as a never-ending sequence of 15 second commercials, text messages, and brief, impersonal encounters. We live in a time when the instant of this present moment is experienced as the sum of all things and the measure of all meaning.

Our focus on the present moment has resulted in a loss of perspective on our world and on our own lives. Our focus on the present has caused us to lose sight of the past and the future as connected with this moment in time. Our loss of our past, our ignorance of history, our abandonment of a heritage creates the impression that this present time is the result of our efforts—the product of our time and energy. Implicitly we think that there was nothing before we were born and that there will be nothing after we have died. We tend to think that the whole meaning of history is disclosed in this present moment. And so we are impatient and find it difficult to wait.

THE DISCIPLINE OF WAITING

But Israel had learned the discipline of waiting. Waiting patiently; waiting longingly; even waiting noisily at times—for their laments to God in the period of waiting were loud and strong! That's part of what we learn from the first verses of Matthew.

In their waiting, Israel discovered the possibility of hope. They learned what hope is precisely because they had to wait. Hope was kept alive in their waiting. Through the discipline of waiting, Israel learned that not everything is determined in a moment, in an hour, a day, a month or years. They learned that God works in God's time and that the human response is to wait. After all, Abraham and Sarah had to wait for 25 years after the first promise of blessing before they would see that blessing fulfilled in the birth of Isaac. Never mind the fact that Abraham was 75 years old and Sarah was 65 years old when the promise was made and waiting for 25 years would make them 100 and 90 years old when Isaac was born! In between the promise and its fulfillment, they showed both faith and doubt; they lamented and schemed; but most of all they waited—in hope! Sometimes patiently; other times impatiently. But they waited nonetheless. No matter what they did, they could not hurry God.

Israel had to wait in Egypt for 400 years before God raised up Moses to lead them out of slavery. They suffered deeply; life was miserable; generations passed. They cried out in despair and perhaps even lost sight of God at times. Certainly their memories of God had faded considerably by the time God responded. But they waited nonetheless. They had no choice.

In the time of the prophets, they too waited. The prophets foresaw a new day and a new time—a day when the poor and the oppressed would be set free; a day when God would show up and do something rather than sit silently in the heavens and observe the suffering of the poor. They were impatient to see that time come. But they waited for years, decades, and centuries. Sometimes they lamented; sometimes they pleaded with God; sometimes they simply were silent. But they waited—in hope.

And in the time of Joseph and Mary, the Jews were once again subjected to the cruel rule of a foreign oppressor—this time the Romans. They had struggled for freedom; some took up arms in vain efforts to set themselves free. But the failure of armed revolt forced them to wait and to hope.

For more than 2000 years the Church has waited for the return of Jesus. In the earliest years after the resurrection and ascension of Jesus, Christians anticipated that he would return very soon. They thought that the wait they would have to endure was only a matter of a few days, then a few months, and at most a few years. But now, 2000 years later we are still waiting—in hope.

One might think that the act of waiting is a waste of time; that it is characterized only by inactivity and resignation to something one cannot change. But nothing could be farther from the truth in the case of Israel. Israel's waiting rarely was a sign of resignation. It often was accompanied by active lament and crying out to God. It was a vigorous, lively waiting. Reread the stories of Abraham and Sarah, the exodus and the prophets to see this. The Israelites were not passive sufferers or waiters!

WAITING LEADS TO HOPE

But in the midst of this waiting Israel discovered something really quite marvelous. Waiting can lead to hope and joy. If we never wait for anything, if we never struggle for anything, if everything comes our way easily and instantly, we can never really learn the discipline of hope. For if our dreams are fulfilled instantly, if our problems are resolved in a moment, if our goals are achieved speedily, how do we learn to live in hope? How do we even know what hope is?

Similarly if we only sing songs of praise all the time, how do we know what real joy is? Waiting and hoping—deep longing and trust in God for the future—create space for real joy, not the substitute, manufactured, fraudulent joy that characterizes so much of our lives and worship. Hope and joy are the products of our waiting!

It is this hope sprung to life that the New Testament's stories of the birth of Jesus express. It is an extravagant hope; it may even be an unreasonable hope. But waiting, hope, and rejoicing must go together. For the ground of hope is to be found not in ourselves, or in the power of those around us, but in our God. And God teaches us how to rejoice by causing us to wait in hope.

It is in this spirit that the Apostle Paul could write in Romans, "...we also boast in our sufferings, knowing that suffering produces endurance, and endurance produces character, and character produces hope, and hope does not disappoint us, because God's love has been poured into our hearts through the Holy Spirit that has been given to us" (Romans 5:3-5).

Advent is a time of waiting. It is a time of preparation. It takes time for us to learn the meaning of the birth of Christ. But we rush to sing Christmas carols too soon, because we do not know how to wait in hope. We rush to the manger without waiting to journey through Advent, the time of waiting. And in the process we lose sight of the long wait that led to hope and the deep longing that leads to joy when it is at last fulfilled.

The genealogy with which Matthew opens reminds us that waiting is a large part of the life of the Church. Waiting for God...waiting for the coming of Christ...waiting for the kingdom of heaven to be established in its fullness.

Chapter 2: A Family Story

Matthew 1:1-17

We have a fascination with family histories. Parents and grandparents pass on family stories to their children and grandchildren. As public records are digitized, people are turning increasingly to online genealogical sites to explore their family history through multiple generations. One of the most recent developments is the wide availability of DNA analysis that will reveal our genetic genealogy. All of this raises a basic question, "Why is our family story so important to us?"

GENEALOGIES TELL OUR STORY

The answer is both simple and profound: knowing our family stories and our genealogical history helps us to understand who we are and our place in the world. It helps us to see ourselves not merely as isolated individuals, but more importantly as part of a broad stream of history. It connects us to a larger story that transcends the minutiae of our daily lives. It helps to give our lives some meaning beyond our solitary existence.

The Bible includes a number of genealogies which help to connect the biblical story. The first biblical genealogy is found in Genesis 5 where we read about wondrously long lives. Reading it can be a cure for insomnia. The list of names and the rhythm of "begetting" one generation after another can quickly become monotonous unless we step back to ask what the point is. Then we begin to see the larger importance of the list of names from generation to generation.

This same principle is true of the genealogy with which Matthew opens his account of the life and ministry of Jesus. It begins with the same words that open the genealogy in Genesis 5. The three sets of fourteen generations included in Matthew's genealogy are not primarily written as an historical account. There are sections of the genealogy where scholars think that a number of generations have been omitted. More importantly, the genealogy in Matthew 1 situates the story of Jesus that Matthew will tell within the larger flow of the story of God and Israel. By locating Abraham at the beginning of the genealogy and Jesus at its end, Matthew makes the point that this overarching history of God's people finds its fulfillment in the birth of Jesus. Through the genealogy Matthew wastes no time providing his readers with the key to a proper understanding of the story he is going to share with us.

In the opening verse of his Gospel, Matthew sets out the claims that he and the early Christian Church put forward regarding Jesus. He wants there to be no mistake: Jesus is the Christ or Messiah. He is God's anointed, the agent of God who will carry out God's purposes. With roots going all the way back to the glorious reign of King David, the hope for a "messiah" (or one who was anointed to a task or role) was grounded in the memory of David's glory. Within the Judaism of Matthew's time, this would have pointed to a series of expectations associated with the coming of Messiah that will be worked out throughout the Gospel of Matthew. The coming of Jesus, Matthew claims, is not a random act of God. It is part of a much larger, much longer history. For Matthew, getting this right is critical. Everything that follows in the Gospel hinges upon the truth of this claim.

SON OF ABRAHAM, SON OF DAVID

The messianic mission of Jesus is reinforced by the two remaining descriptions of Jesus in Matt 1:1. Jesus is described as "son of David, son of Abraham." The assertion that Jesus is the son of David was an essential requirement for the Messiah. Jesus is the long-awaited descendant of David who will fulfill God's promises to David that he would always have a descendant to occupy the throne of Israel (2 Samuel 7).

By identifying Jesus as a "son of Abraham" Matthew associates Jesus with the entire history of Israel and especially with the promises that God made to Abraham in Gen 12:1-3. Key among these is the promise that through Abraham *"all the families of the earth* shall be blessed" (Gen 12:3b; emphasis added). The mission of Jesus reaches beyond the boundaries of Israel. With this reference to Abraham right at the beginning of his Gospel, Matthew begins to prepare his readers for the climactic extension of the mission of Jesus and the Church to "go and make disciples of all nations..." (Matt 28:19).

What we see, then, is that these opening verses of Matthew, rather than being a throw away heading for the Gospel, actually provide us with the lenses through which to read the rest of the story of Jesus. This is the story of Jesus the Messiah, truly son of Abraham and truly son of David, who draws together and fulfills the promises made to Abraham and David centuries earlier. That's an important point to make in a world in which the evidence might suggest that God's plans have changed or that they have failed. By linking the story of Jesus with the entire history of the Jewish people, Matthew announces the coming of Jesus Christ as the fulfillment of God's plan. With subtlety, but with force, Matthew stakes out his claim. It will be contested within the Gospel as some reject Jesus as the Christ; but there will be others who accept him. Not much has changed: in our day, the Church's claims about Jesus continue to be contested. That is the reality of claims about Jesus. It is only with eyes of faith that we too can come to confess Jesus as the Christ, son of David and son of Abraham.

Chapter 3: Surprising Ancestors

Matthew 1:2-17

There's one in every family. You know what I mean. We all have at least one relative who is an embarrassment to the rest of the family. It may be an awkward cousin, an overbearing parent, a prickly aunt or some relative who has committed an act so scandalous to the family that we don't even mention him or her. As much as we might try to gloss over the embarrassment, it is still there, reminding us that families have their secrets.

FOUR UNEXPECTED ANCESTORS

The genealogy of Jesus that Matthew presents to us is comprised mostly of names that don't jump out at us. Of course there are the noteworthy. Abraham and David stand head and shoulders above the rest. Then there's Isaac, Jacob, and Solomon. But most of the names in the genealogy are forgettable, if not forgotten. Hezron, Aminadab, and Eliad among them. Astonishingly, among the men who dominate the list of descendants of Abraham and ancestors of Jesus we find four women. Sarah, Rebekah, Rachel, and Leah might be prime candidates for inclusion if gender balance were an issue. Instead we find Tamar, Rahab, Ruth, and the wife of Uriah. Since women don't often make it into genealogies in the man's world that was biblical Israel, what's even more startling, perhaps, is that *these* four women made the list. For each of them, in her own way, had some scent of scandal about her.

TAMAR

The story of Tamar is a sordid affair. In Genesis 38 we learn that Tamar married the eldest son of Judah only to have him die before they had a son. When, according to the levirate custom, Judah's second son married Tamar to ensure the continuation of the eldest son's lineage, he too died. Judah refused to give Tamar his third son, fearing that he too would die. But Tamar was determined to provide a son for her dead husband. One day she went out in disguise to meet Judah. He mistook her for a prostitute and had sexual relations with her. The resulting pregnancy, of course, would raise questions about the widow Tamar's character. When she was brought before Judah accused of immorality and in danger of being executed, Tamar revealed the fact that her pregnancy was the result of the actions of her father-in-law. Having been confronted with the truth, Judah confessed that Tamar was more righteous than he had been, since she had been determined to fulfill her responsibilities according to the levirate custom while Judah had withheld his third son from Tamar (Gen 38:26). Isn't it surprising that in a genealogy that is written to establish the pedigree of Jesus as the son of Abraham and the son of David, we find Tamar whose story could be so embarrassing to the family?

RAHAB

The story of Rahab in Joshua 2 and 6 is, perhaps, a little less sordid; but it still makes her inclusion in Matthew's genealogy surprising. Rahab was a Canaanite, dwelling in the city of Jericho. She also was a prostitute. For Israel, these two facts marked her as an outsider. But when the Israelite spies arrived in Jericho to scout out the city, Rahab took them in and hid them from the agents of the king of Jericho. Prior to making their escape possible through a window in her home, Rahab negotiated safety for her family and herself when the Israelites came to capture the city. After the destruction of Jericho and the rescue of Rahab and her family, she lived in Israel for the rest of her life. A Canaanite prostitute living in the midst of Israel found her way into the genealogy of Jesus. What a surprise!

RUTH THE MOABITE

Then there's Ruth the Moabite who married an Israelite. When Ruth's husband died, she moved to Israel with her mother-in-law Naomi. Now, as a refugee living in a foreign land and as a widow, Ruth was especially vulnerable. Ruth was *persona non grata*. She had no legal standing in Israel. Scouring the field of an Israelite landowner for some small portion of food to survive, Ruth encountered Boaz. Ultimately, Ruth and Boaz were married and she became part of the Israelite community. A Moabite woman who had been incorporated into the people of Israel is included as the great-grandmother of King David. Wouldn't there be good reason to hide this?

THE WIFE OF URIAH

Finally, there's the "wife of Uriah" who is not even mentioned by her name in the genealogy. The story of David's illicit affair with the wife of Uriah in 2 Samuel 11-12 is as disgraceful a story as one can find in the Bible or beyond it. Abusing his royal power, David first overpowered Bathsheba, the wife of Uriah the Hittite and then, to cover up his adultery, had ensured that Uriah would be killed in battle. We don't know whether Bathsheba was an Israelite or not, but we do know that the mere mention of her as the wife of Uriah would call to mind all the details of David's greatest sin. Yet, there she is, right in the spotlight again in the genealogy of Jesus!

WHY THESE FOUR WOMEN?

The presence of these women in Matthew's genealogy makes me wonder, what was the point? What was Matthew trying to say about Jesus by including these women? A couple of things come to mind.

First of all, since several of these women were not Israelites, we might conclude that Matthew was foreshadowing the mission of Jesus that would extend beyond the boundaries of Israel to include Gentiles within the people of God. Jesus's Jewish and royal pedigree was established in the genealogy; but that pedigree had some startling features. Ethnic purity was not part of the plan. Rather, as Jesus commissioned his disciples at the end of the Gospel of Matthew to go into all the world (Matthew 28:16-20), so here at the beginning of the story we find the nations represented in his genealogy.

Second, several of the women had backgrounds that would be scandalous in that world, if not in ours. Their sexual activities were outside the boundaries of what was acceptable in polite society. Including prostitutes in the list of ancestors certainly was an embarrassment to the genealogy. But here we nevertheless find Rahab and even Tamar. Adultery—not to mention murder—was condemned and yet we find the wife of Uriah in the family tree. A Moabite widow—a refugee—is the great grandmother of David! But in spite of these irregularities, these women are included in the genealogy. The family tree of Jesus includes the outcast, the socially disadvantaged and those who might be thought to be scandalous. Matthew was reminding us that the mission and message of Jesus embraces those who are disadvantaged socially and economically. Even a refugee such as Ruth finds a place. The Gospel has a wide embrace!

Finally, the genealogy of Jesus casts the disputes Jesus has with those who oppose him throughout Matthew in a new light. No longer is it sufficient simply to maintain longstanding prejudices. The Gospel transforms society, breaking down uncrossable barriers to establish a new people of God. The Church does not follow in the way of Jesus when it builds walls to keep out the weak, the poor, the scandalous, or the sinner. They have a place in the genealogy of Jesus and they have a place in the kingdom of God.

Chapter 4: Righteous Joseph

Matthew 1:18-25

Matthew's account of the birth of Jesus in Matthew 1:18–25 has one primary concern: to establish the identity and mission of Jesus from the very beginning of his story. For Matthew, Jesus is the Messiah or Christ (Matthew 1:18), the agent of God who will establish God's kingdom and save his people from their sins (Matthew 1:21).

AN UNEXPECTED PREGNANCY

Behind these overarching claims made by Matthew is a very human story involving a young couple: Joseph and Mary. Matthew grounds his lofty message about Jesus's identity and mission as the Christ in the earthiness and complexities of human life. It doesn't get much earthier than a pregnancy out of wedlock, especially in the society of Joseph and Mary. Put that together with the fact that the young couple had not yet had sexual intercourse and you have the makings of a real potboiler.

Joseph and Mary were betrothed to one another. According to the customs of their day, this meant that they were committed to marriage. In many ways they already were considered to be husband and wife, except that Mary had not yet gone to live with Joseph and they had not yet had sexual intercourse. That would occur sometime in the near future.

While this story has the potential to become quite bawdy, the characters in the story draw our attention in another direction. Mary's pregnancy and the statement that Joseph and Mary had not yet had intercourse forced Joseph to the conclusion that Mary had been unfaithful to him. Under the terms of the Torah, a woman who was found unfaithful was to be punished. In earlier times, the Torah would have required a death sentence for Mary. But by Joseph's time, most rabbis required a lesser penalty, including divorce and public shaming.

A RIGHTEOUS MAN

Matthew portrays Joseph as a righteous man who confronted a significant dilemma. We usually understand the description of Joseph as "righteous" to mean that he was a good man, a kind man. But Joseph's "righteousness" in this context has a specific meaning: it refers to Joseph's thorough adherence to the law, the Torah. Joseph was a devout, practising Jew. His decision to divorce Mary was the right one according to the law.

But Matthew tells us more about Joseph. He notes that while Joseph had decided to sever his relationship with Mary, in accordance with the law and the custom of his time, he had decided to do so "quietly," evidently to reduce Mary's public disgrace. Joseph had found a way to be faithful to the requirements of the law, but to do so in a respectful and sensitive manner. Joseph attempted to strike a remarkable balance between righteousness and compassion.

However, Joseph's righteousness became even more startling when, after the appearance of an angel in a dream, he abandoned adherence to the law by accepting the angel's exhortation to take Mary as his wife. In this extraordinary situation, Joseph's righteousness transcended the letter of the law. Even Joseph's attempt to lessen the public impact of the divorce upon Mary was not enough. For Joseph, being righteous no longer meant blind, literal adherence to the Torah; the instruction from the angel trumped the law. The imminent arrival of Jesus somehow transformed the righteousness expected of Joseph. This is a theme that Jesus will articulate again and again later in Matthew: there is a righteousness greater than rigid adherence to the law. Sometimes adherence to the letter of the law causes us to lose sight of the heart and soul of the law's intention. Sometimes the greater righteousness is not only love for God, but love for our neighbour.

I am certain that it was not easy for Joseph to set aside his decision to divorce Mary as was expected in the custom of his society. Such a decision would bring the scent of scandal upon him too. But Joseph demonstrated his righteousness by seeing and hearing beyond the law of his day to the word of the Lord spoken through the angel. That's much more difficult than following a rulebook. It requires attentive listening for the voice of God.

Chapter 5: Jesus, Son of God

Matthew 1:18-25

Sometimes pregnancies come as a surprise. Perhaps they shouldn't—but they do. In the case of Mary, her pregnancy was a shock!

In these verses Matthew makes two important claims. First, Jesus was conceived in Mary's womb "from the Holy Spirit" (verses 18, 20). Second, Joseph and Mary had not had sexual intercourse prior to Jesus's conception (verse 18) and did not do so until after the birth of Jesus (verse 25) even though Joseph and Mary were married prior to Jesus's birth. Given our social and intellectual context in a society in which scientific knowledge reigns supreme, we can get bogged down with questions about whether such a conception is even possible. But for Matthew, these claims reach beyond what is verifiable either scientifically or historically; they go to the very heart of the Gospel because they reflect the evangelist's conviction that Jesus is the Son of God.

Matthew is quite aware that the claims he makes about the origin of Jesus are remarkable, even extraordinary. With our tendency to rule out the extraordinary from the realm of history, we are left seeking some explanation to support Matthew's claims. But by doing so I think we often miss the importance of what Matthew says. Our focus turns away from the good news of Jesus to seek justification for that good news. In the process, I think we miss the point.

TRULY THE SON OF GOD

The dual claim Matthew makes that Jesus was conceived "from the Holy Spirit" and that Mary and Joseph had not had sexual relations is marshalled in order to establish Matthew's supreme claim that Jesus is truly the Son of God. One might assert that as every kingly descendent of David was given the title "son of God" at the time of his coronation (see 2 Samuel 7:14; Psalms 2:7) the designation of Jesus as the Messiah, the long-awaited Davidic king, was sufficient to establish his status as a "son of God." But for Matthew and the early Church Jesus was not simply a "son of God" in this derivative sense, a status that he shared with every king in Jerusalem descended from David. Rather, Jesus's divine sonship is qualitatively different. Yes, he is a "son of David" and therefore rightly can claim the title "son of God." But Matthew, by asserting that Jesus was conceived "from the Holy Spirit" presses forward an astounding claim: Jesus is *the* Son of God, begotten through the agency of the Holy Spirit and born of the Virgin Mary. His divine sonship is fundamentally different. The recognition of this is a major concern of Matthew. It is for this reason that at the time of his baptism, a voice from heaven announces over Jesus, "This is my Son, the Beloved, with whom I am well pleased" (Matthew 3:17). The same pronouncement is made over Jesus at the time of the transfiguration (Matthew 17:5). Finally, at his crucifixion, a Roman centurion, having observed the manner of Jesus's death exclaims, "Truly this man was God's Son!" (Matthew 27:54).

25

Throughout his Gospel, Matthew proclaims that Jesus is the unique Son of God.

NOT EVERYONE ACCEPTS MATTHEW'S CLAIM

But, of course, not everyone recognizes or accepts Matthew's claim. The Gospel is filled with characters who reject Jesus as Messiah and Son of God. This should not surprise us. For confessing Jesus as the Son of God makes a claim upon us. In Matthew, the claims placed upon those who would call Jesus "Lord" are weighty. It is not sufficient to mouth the words, "Jesus is Lord." As Jesus says in Matthew 7:21, "Not everyone who says to me, 'Lord, Lord,' will enter the kingdom of heaven, but only the one who does the will of my Father in heaven." Recognizing Jesus as the Son of God means receiving his words as the words of God; it means accepting his instruction as coming from the Father in heaven; and it means submitting ourselves to the salvation brought through Jesus.

Matthew's assertion that Jesus is the Son of God is fundamental to his Gospel and to the teaching of the Church. It is only the Son of God who can save his people from their sins. The early Church was convinced that we humans are so enmeshed in our sinfulness that only God can extricate us from the web of sin. So Matthew's claim that Jesus is the Son of God stands at the heart of the good news. Without this, we believe in vain and as the Apostle Paul would say in another context, "we are of all people most to be pitied" (1 Corinthians 15:19).

Chapter 6: Jesus, Son of Joseph

Matthew 1:18-25

Matthew and the early Church had a problem. How could Jesus be the son of Joseph and therefore a descendant of David if Mary's pregnancy was not the result of sexual intercourse between Mary and Joseph? If Jesus was not the (biological) son of Joseph, then we might conclude that he could not be a descendant of David, and therefore was disqualified from being the Messiah. Matthew provides us with his answer to this question.

JOSEPH'S ADOPTED SON

Fundamentally, Matthew asserts that Jesus was the legal son of Joseph by adoption. This assertion is supported by Matthew in a couple of ways. First of all, while Joseph's initial decision to divorce Mary quietly would have been the correct one according to tradition, his obedience to the instruction received from the angel in effect made him the father of Jesus. But more importantly, by following the second part of the angel's instruction to give Jesus his name, Joseph asserted his status as the legal father of Jesus. Naming was the prerogative of the father and therefore by giving Jesus his name, Joseph became the father of Jesus and Jesus became a descendant of David. Finally, through the rest of Mathew's nativity narrative, Joseph acted as Jesus's father by heeding the warning of the angel and protecting both Mary and Jesus by removing them to Egypt. He also brought them back to their homeland once the threat from Herod had subsided. Joseph acted fully as the father of Jesus by naming, protecting, and providing for him.

In our thinking Matthew's argument for the paternity of Joseph may be questionable because we tend to focus on the biological paternity. But according to the customs of that time, Jesus would have been considered fully the son of Joseph. Jesus therefore had every right to be called a son of David.

The scandal of Mary's pregnancy out of wedlock has been addressed by Matthew in a thorough way by attributing the conception of Jesus to the Holy Spirit, with the support of an angelic announcement and a righteous man.

SON OF GOD AND SON OF JOSEPH AND MARY

Matthew's account of Jesus's descent, however, has another focus. Matthew asserts that Jesus is fully the son of Mary and, by adoption, the son of Joseph. He is, in other words, a human being. This may seem obvious to us who have read these stories many times. But we must not as a result rush past it. The full humanity of Jesus came to be a central assertion of the Church in its subsequent creeds just as did the full divinity of Jesus as we observed in the previous meditation. It took several centuries of reflection and debate for the Church to embrace the full and complete humanity of Jesus. A tendency to compromise on the humanity of Jesus to protect his status as the Son of God ran deep in some parts of the Church. But, ultimately, the Church embraced the principle that Jesus could redeem only those parts of our humanity which he himself shared with us. If there are elements of our humanity that Jesus does not share with us, then those elements could not have been saved through the work of Christ. Thus the confession of the Church that Jesus is "very man" is critical to our salvation.

Matthew did not have in mind the fully developed Christian understanding of Jesus as fully divine and fully human. That would take centuries to articulate. But we do find in this passage and throughout Matthew the evangelist's witness to Christ which provided the Church with some of the raw materials out of which it would be able to articulate its mature confession of Jesus as "true God from true God" and "truly human." On this confession hangs our salvation.

Chapter 7: A Continuing Story

Matthew 1: 18-25

The opening verses of Matthew's Gospel are filled with references to the journey of Israel with God. The long genealogy which links Jesus to Abraham and David supports the claim that he is the Christ. His conception "through the Holy Spirit" points toward the unique relationship between God the Father and Jesus that unfolds throughout the rest of the Gospel. It is evident through these connections that Matthew (and the early Church) saw a continuing drama unfold from the story of Israel to the story of Jesus and then through the story of the Church. In verses 22-23 Matthew introduces another feature of his reading of the significance of Jesus.

IT ALL GOES BACK TO ABRAHAM

In the Bible, God's determination to bring a lost world back to himself took a dramatic turn in Genesis 12:1-9 when God called

Abraham to leave everything behind and to move toward an uncertain future sustained only by the promises of God. Abraham's obedience provided an antidote to the plague of rebellion that emanated from Eden (Genesis 3-11). Central to God's redemptive purpose was the promise that through Abraham and his descendants all the families of the earth would be blessed (Genesis 12:3). Throughout the Old Testament, Abraham's progeny struggled to fulfil their vocation to bring blessing upon all peoples. It was not easy to live out such a vocation. Life as the people of God was fraught with opportunities to set the vocation aside in favour of self-interest, national interests, and just plain stubbornness. At times Israel needed to be reminded of its divine purpose. But while they may have wavered in the vocation to bless all the families of the earth, God's determination that this should happen never wavered.

FULFILLING THE PROMISE

Matthew interprets the coming of Jesus as the fulfilment of this promise to Abraham, drawing connections between the life of Jesus and the work of God through Abraham and his descendants. Matthew was especially adept at this. He repeatedly points out that what takes place in the birth of Jesus fulfils words spoken by the prophets (Matthew 1:22-23; 2:5-6, 15, 17-18). With his frequent references to the fulfilment of the prophecies of the past, Matthew stresses the continuity of God's purpose in the world. For Matthew, the events of Israel's history and now the events of Jesus's birth are not random. They are the product of the dynamic outworking of God's will in partnership with the faithful response of humans such as Joseph and Mary. Matthew affirms that in the birth of Jesus the mission of God to bring blessing to all the world takes a decisive turn; but it is still the same mission to bring the world back to God that was evident throughout the Old Testament. In the events of Jesus's life, the promises made to Abraham are coming to fruition.

Matthew shares this conviction with other New Testament writers. For example, the Apostle Paul opens his letter to the Romans with a salutation that draws the connection between the words of the prophets and their fulfilment in Jesus. He begins, "Paul, a servant of Jesus Christ, called to be an apostle, set apart for the gospel of God, *which he promised beforehand through his prophets in the holy scriptures*, the gospel concerning his son, who was descended from David according to the flesh and was declared to be Son of God with power according to the spirit of holiness by resurrection from the dead..." (Romans 1:1-4; emphasis added). Both Matthew and Paul understand that the prophets sometimes spoke words that carried meanings deeper and more inspired than even the prophets themselves recognized. They spoke of things beyond their experience and knowledge, beyond their own horizon.

GOD'S CONTINUING WORK

We must understand, however, that Matthew's concern is not to suggest that the prophets of Israel were merely skilled fortune-tellers who could see into the future; he sees something far more enduring in their words. With his references to the fulfilment of the words of the prophets, Matthew asserts that the purposes of God are steady and reliable. In the face of evidence that appears to contradict and call into question the words of the prophets and the purposes of God, Matthew stresses that God is faithful after all! What began with the promises that God made to Abraham comes to a decisive fulfilment in the birth of Jesus. The emphasis in Matthew is placed upon the continuity of God's commitment to work toward the salvation of the world, first through Abraham and his descendants, and now—at last—through his own Son, Jesus Christ.

We often find ourselves in a situation that parallels that of the prophets and the people of Matthew's time. While we might wish to believe that the purposes of God are moving forward, we are confronted with voices and events that call this into question. It is not always easy to perceive the purposes of God that are at work among us and in the world. So we are left with the words of the prophets and the witness of Matthew that God's purposes will prevail, his promises will be kept and the salvation he has provided will be received. It is this strong sense of the continuing work of God that Matthew shares with us as we prepare to celebrate the nativity of Jesus.

Chapter 8: You Shall Name Him "Jesus"

Matthew 1:18-25

Matthew includes nothing in his account of the birth of Jesus that is not important for the overall story that he is telling. This is true especially of the two names that are given to the child conceived in the womb of Mary: Jesus and Immanuel. In this chapter and the next we are going to consider the significance of these names for Matthew and for us.

In his first encounter with the angel of the Lord, Joseph was told to follow through with his marriage to Mary despite the fact that she was pregnant prior to the consummation of their marriage. The child in her womb, he was told, was conceived "from the Holy Spirit." The angel then told Joseph that this child was to be named "Jesus, for he will save his people from their sins" (Matthew 1:21).

WHAT'S IN A NAME?

Biblical names frequently communicated the character and mission of the person named. Thus, for example, the name of the prophet Elijah means "the Lord is my God." Given Elijah's dramatic defense of the worship of the Lord and his uncompromising message that Israel must choose loyalty to the Lord over the worship of other gods, the prophet's name reflects his character and vocation (1 Kings 17–2 Kings 2). Or we could consider the name of Daniel who served in the court of the Babylonian conqueror of Judah. In the face of efforts to extinguish the Jewishness of Daniel and his compatriots, and his subjection to a series of trials, the meaning of Daniel's name—God is my judge—expresses his confidence in the judgment of God over that of the Babylonian king. Walking the tightrope between service to his overlord and devotion to his God, Daniel's life embodied the meaning of his name, recognizing that in truth only God could judge him.

In the case of Jesus, Matthew links the significance of the angel's command to Joseph to give the child this name to the fact that the Greek name "Jesus" actually is a translation of the Hebrew name "Joshua" which means "the Lord saves." Naming the child "Jesus" conveys the mission that God gives to him—"he will save his people from their sins."

Coming at the beginning of the Gospel, the full meaning of the name "Jesus" unfolds only as the story progresses. In Matthew, the saving activity of Jesus takes several forms. For example, when Jesus and his disciples got into a boat and set sail, a storm caught up to them and threatened to sink the boat. Jesus was sound asleep. The disciples, however, were gripped with fear and cried out to Jesus, "Lord, *save us*! We are perishing!" (Matthew 8:25; emphasis added). Jesus then stilled the stormy wind. In this scene, the plea of the disciples has a very specific meaning: save us from our immediate physical peril. But in Matthew we have to read this story in the light of the name given to Jesus in 1:21 and acknowledge that "salvation" comes in many ways and circumstances.

In the very next chapter Jesus has an encounter with a woman who has been afflicted for twelve years (Matthew 9:20-22). Surreptitiously the woman touches Jesus's clothing, having come to believe that, "If I simply touch his clothes I shall *be saved*" (author's translation). While many English translations speak of the woman being "made well," the Greek uses the verb "to be saved." Then in his response to the woman, Jesus says, "Take heart, woman; your faith *has saved you*" (author's translation). The story concludes with the statement that instantly the woman *was saved.* For Matthew, this is not simply a story about a random healing; Matthew's choice of language makes it clear that the healing of the woman is an act of salvation brought by Jesus.

Later still, in another scene on the water, Jesus invites Peter to join him in walking on the water. Initially successful, Peter suddenly begins to sink and cries out, "Lord, *save me!*" (Matthew 14:30; emphasis added). Of course, Jesus does and the episode concludes with Peter's exclamation, "Truly you are the Son of God" (Matthew 14:33).

WHAT KIND OF SALVATION?

These three episodes display the scope of Matthew's vision of the salvation that Jesus brings. Yet in the naming of Jesus, the angel provides a very specific interpretation of the meaning of Jesus's name: "he will save his people from their sins." The salvation of people from their sins clearly is fundamental to the mission of Jesus. As Matthew illustrates later in his story, Jesus's messianic mission is not the overthrow of Roman rule or the establishment of a political kingdom. For Matthew, Jesus's mission to give his life as a ransom for many (Matthew 20:28) is fundamental. The image of a ransom being paid builds upon the practice of debt-slavery in which a person who could not pay a debt could be forced into slavery. This bondage often was irreversible since the enslaved individual had little opportunity to repay the debt. But if someone offered to pay the debt, then the freedom of the slave could be secured. Therefore in Matthew 20:28 Jesus's mission is to give his life as a ransom, to pay the debt owed by many. Their freedom is at stake. From what are they being ransomed? From the power of sin and the guilt of their sins.

This is confirmed later in the scene at the Last Supper when Jesus breaks the bread and shares the cup of wine with his disciples saying, "Drink from it, all of you; for this is my blood of the covenant, which is poured out for many *for the forgiveness of sins*" (Matthew 26:27-28; emphasis added). This is the language of sacrifice in which the breaking of the body of Jesus and the shedding of his blood is understood as a sacrificial act to secure forgiveness for sins. This is language that Jesus's disciples and Matthew's readers would have recognized immediately as drawing upon the Old Testament's provisions for the forgiveness of sins through the sacrificial system. In the life of the Church, it became language that was repeated whenever the sacrifice of Jesus was celebrated (see for example, 1 Corinthians 11:23-26).

SALVATION FROM THEIR SINS

By linking the mission of Jesus with his name at the very beginning of his Gospel, Matthew foreshadows how the story of Jesus will unfold. He anticipates the mission of Jesus that will be expressed using several different images. Matthew already has introduced Jesus as the Messiah or Christ, the son of David. As we shall see, a cornerstone of Matthew's interpretation of Jesus's arrival is that it marks the coming of the kingdom of heaven. Here Matthew introduces a sacrificial image in which the very name of Jesus articulates his mission to "save his people from their sins." He points us, in the first chapter of his story of Jesus, toward the final chapters in which he recounts the sacrificial death of Jesus as a ransom for many. Therefore, according to Matthew, the mission of Jesus was not primarily political, military, social, or economic. It has implications for each of these spheres; but fundamentally, the coming of Jesus was to save his people from their sins.

Chapter 9: Immanuel – God is with Us

Matthew 1: 18-25

The prophet Isaiah lived in tumultuous times. Events unfolding on the world stage were having a dire impact upon the tiny kingdom of Judah with its capital city in Jerusalem. The year was approximately 735 BCE. On the horizon, the Assyrian Empire was stirring from its slumber and had designs on the small kingdoms of the area. The Syrians with their capital in Damascus and the northern Israelite kingdom with its capital in Samaria had decided that the best defense against the Assyrian threat would be the formation of an alliance between Syria, Israel, and Judah. The only problem was that King Ahaz of Judah did not want to join the alliance. Faced with his resistance, the kings of Syria and Israel decided to force Judah to join them. Amassing their armies on the border of Judah, just a short distance from Jerusalem, the shock waves rippled through the capital city. The prophet Isaiah advised King Ahaz against any rash actions, either against the alliance or in the direction of requesting Assyrian protection. His message was simple: trust the Lord to protect Jerusalem and Judah. After all, Isaiah was firmly behind the tradition that God had promised David that he would always have a descendant to rule in Jerusalem and that since the Temple was the dwelling place of the Lord, God would not permit the city to fall to an enemy. But Ahaz had difficulty hearing Isaiah's message in the face of the superior forces of Syria and Israel. The immediacy of the threatening posture of his neighbours seemed to trump any encouragement from Isaiah. After all, a prophet might have the luxury of making vague, impractical speeches but a king has to make decisions in the real world. Kings take action, give orders, and deploy their armies. Trusting and waiting for God isn't in their repertoire.

A CHILD'S NAME

It was in the midst of this crisis that Isaiah uttered one of his most famous and most confusing sayings. In Isaiah 7, in an effort to stress to King Ahaz that the threat from the kings of Syria and Israel was fleeting, the prophet said that by the time a young woman (virgin) could conceive, give birth to a son and that child could know the difference between right and wrong, the threat would dissipate. The name of the child is critical, "Immanuel" – "God is with us." This, of course, had been Isaiah's message all along. God is with us, not only in the Temple and in the affairs of religion, but also in the affairs of state. The message of Immanuel affirmed that God rules over even the mighty kings in whose shadow King Ahaz shook like a leaf caught in a gale force wind. In the face of the contingencies and crises of everyday life, King Ahaz could have acted with the assurance that "God is with us." What a difference that would have made. But instead he sent to Assyria for help and submitted to their control. Isaiah's message fell on deaf ears.

When Matthew drew upon the text from Isaiah 7 to witness to the significance of Jesus's coming the times were no less perilous. The Jewish people now lived under the tyranny of Rome. Roman power could bring order, but it also could bring violence and oppression. Herod the Great governed under the watchful eye of the Romans. He was known for his brutality and ruthlessness. While some benefitted from this power arrangement, most Jews lived under the burden of Roman and Herodian rule. What would they have heard when Matthew claimed that the birth of Jesus is a sign that "God is with us"? For Matthew this name adds another layer to what he has already said about Jesus: he is son of Abraham and son of David; he is the Christ (Messiah); he was conceived through the Holy Spirit and therefore is Son of God; and now he is Immanuel, "God with us."

GOD IS WITH US – STILL!

It is important that both in its original introduction by the prophet Isaiah and in its appropriation by Matthew the name is used in contexts of conflict and uncertainty. The affirmation that God is with us provides a basis on which we can be assured of God's continuing presence, provision and protection, even in the most uncertain of situations. At one level the naming of Immanuel is a Christological statement, reinforcing Matthew's understanding of Jesus as the Son of God. But at another level, the presence of Jesus is a visible and concrete sign that God has drawn near to God's people. They are no longer alone. The long period of waiting is ending. Not everyone will be able to see this. King Herod does not perceive the truth of Immanuel; he sees only a threat. But for those who read Matthew's Gospel with eyes of faith, we can once again live out of the promise and presence that arises from the name given to Jesus: Immanuel—God is with us.

Chapter 10: A Star is Born

Matthew 2:1-12

In Matthew 1 the Evangelist establishes the broad strokes of Jesus's identity as the Messiah who is both the Son of God and the son of Joseph. The genealogy that Matthew provides makes this abundantly clear (1:1-17). Then, once this groundwork is laid, the focus turns to Joseph and Mary (1:18-25). In Matthew's account, the plans of heaven are translated into the everyday lives of two young Jews. In this instance these plans are messy. Mary's unexpected and unorthodox pregnancy created turmoil that was resolved only by an angelic intervention and Joseph's willingness to follow the instructions he received.

The final verses of Matthew 1 announce the birth of Jesus rather blandly. In contrast to Luke's account of Jesus's nativity (Luke 2:6-7), Matthew provides no details. Here there are no swaddling clothes, no angel choirs, no bleating sheep and no lowing cattle; there is just the unadorned statement that Jesus was born and a notation that Joseph named him as he had been instructed. If Jesus's lineage and conception are exceptional, his birth certainly is mundane. That is, until we read the opening verses of the next chapter with the appearance of a star, the entrance of wise men, and the introduction of a tyrannical king.

As Matthew 2 opens, our attention moves away from the domestic drama of a young couple to a more public sphere. What had been a family affair creating a domestic crisis of sorts, now generates public shockwaves. Matthew intentionally draws a connection between the events in Bethlehem and the larger stage of Jerusalem and the kingdom of Herod the Great.

A STAR APPEARS

The action in Matthew 2 is prompted by the appearance of a star in the sky. People are fascinated by signs and wonders in the sky. A solar eclipse, a shooting star, and a bright comet in the night sky all can draw a crowd to gaze upward. Still today we marvel at these astronomical occurrences even though we explain them scientifically. But in the world of Matthew when such scientific explanations were not available, people read much more into these changes in the sky. Sudden changes could portend good or ill. They were significant because they were interpreted as wonders that overflowed with meaning. Such phenomena peeled back the heavens to reveal information normally unavailable to humans. They were understood to reveal a deeper meaning for events and to open the way to a vision into the future. In this case, the wise men read the signs and drew their conclusion.

Some have tried to identify scientifically an astronomical incident that would correspond with the timing of Matthew's account of the appearance of a star in the sky and therefore confirm the historicity of what he tells us. A number of theories have been proposed. But the results of such inquiries have been contested at best. This should neither surprise us nor be a serious problem for readers of Matthew, however. For we trust this narrative not because historians and scientists can confirm the appearance of the star scientifically or according to the canons of modern historiography, but rather because in the scriptures we, along with generations of the faithful before us, hear the Word of God. This is part of our faith.

WHAT DOES THIS MEAN?

We should not be surprised, then, that when the wise men of Matthew 2 saw a new star in the night sky they interpreted it to signal that something new was taking place. The wise men or magi mentioned by Matthew likely were astrologers from Persia or Babylon who may well have been in demand as advisers to the leaders of their society. They were star gazers who read into the changes in the night sky signs about events that were unfolding or that were about to occur. So when the star mentioned by Matthew appeared, the wise men discerned that this signified the birth of a new king of the Jews. We are not told how or why they arrived at this conclusion. They just did.

Magi had a tainted reputation among Jews and later among Christians. They were viewed with suspicion in part because the Old Testament condemns all practices of divination (Deuteronomy 18:9-14) in favour of prophecy as the means by which God would speak to God's people. Astrologers also were suspect because for many other peoples the stars, the sun, and the moon were viewed as gods with some measure of influence over events of the world; and of course this ran counter to the teaching of Judaism and Christianity.

THE FIRST TO BOW BEFORE JESUS

It is surprising, then, that the first people in Matthew's gospel to recognize the significance of Jesus's birth are not Jews, but rather exotic easterners from Persia or Babylon whose practices would have been met with disdain, fear, and curiosity. These outsiders were more receptive to the birth of the Son of God than were Jesus's own people. According to Matthew's account, these wise men were the first to bow before the newborn king of the Jews (Matthew 2:11).

By presenting the magi in this way, Matthew foreshadows what we read later in his Gospel. There we find that while most of Jesus's own ministry was directed toward Jews, the commission he gave to the disciples and the Church after his resurrection is to take the gospel to all nations (28:16–20). The nations will demonstrate a receptivity and openness to Jesus that had failed to materialize among his own people. We get the first hint of this openness here in the form of the wise men.

Chapter 11: The Treachery Begins

Matthew 2:1-12

E nglish translations of Matthew 2 frequently are misleading when they say that the magi saw the star "in the east." When we think about it, if the magi were *from the east* and the star appeared *in the eastern sky*, then in their quest to follow the star they would have travelled further east—exactly the opposite direction from Jerusalem! For this reason, with a better translation of the Greek, it is more likely that in their conversation with King Herod the wise men refer to having seen the star "at its rising," that is, when it appeared.

The star's appearance prompted the magi to travel to Jerusalem in search of a newborn king of the Jews. The inquiries made by the wise men probably were innocent enough. "Where is the child who has been born king of the Jews? For we observed his star at its rising, and have come to pay him homage." Jerusalem was the logical place to make these inquiries. For all they knew, the child was born into Herod's royal household, an heir to the throne rather than a pretender to the throne. It's only in light of the fact that Herod and those around him knew nothing about such a royal birth that the inquiries created such a stir in Jerusalem. For the always suspicious Herod this could signal only one thing: a plot to overthrow him.

A careful reading of Matthew 2 reveals that the wise men did not necessarily seek out King Herod in order to find this young heir to the throne. The biblical text only says that they asked where the king would be born, not indicating to whom this question was addressed. Perhaps they simply asked around. They may have sought out various leaders in Jerusalem, perhaps even religious leaders. Somehow, word about the arrival of the wise men and their inquiries made its way to the King. Herod himself was shaken by the rumour that wise men had come seeking a new king of the Jews because they had seen a star in the sky. Such news was not welcome because Herod always was on the alert for potential threats to his position. With Herod on edge, all of Jerusalem was gripped with trepidation.

THE PRETENDER KING

Herod the Great who ruled from 37-4 BC was a notorious tyrant. He came to power with Roman support and as a result of conflict and intrigue. He was an Idumean Jew rather than from the tribe of Judah and therefore did not have the pedigree of David to support his claim to be king of the Jews. (The contrast with Jesus's lineage as outlined in Matthew 1 should not be lost on readers of the first gospel.) Herod gained power because of his skill in cultivating relationships with whoever was in power in Rome and because of his willingness to do whatever was necessary to secure his position. While Herod is well known for his reconstruction of the Temple in

Jerusalem and his reinforcement of the mighty mountaintop fortress at Masada, he is perhaps even better known as a ruthless ruler whose reign was characterized by brutal treatment of any whom he suspected of being opposed to his reign. Herod even murdered members of his own family because he suspected them of treachery against him, sometimes with little or no evidence.

THE PARANOID KING

Matthew's description of the fear that struck King Herod upon hearing that the wise men brought news of the birth of a king of the Jews is entirely consistent with what we know about Herod. Such a rumour immediately would have been met with suspicion and apprehension. The fear that filled the city of Jerusalem may have been because Herod's supporters would have shared his anxiety over the birth of a new king, or it may have been fear among the population that such a rumour would trigger yet another round of violent and unpredictable behaviour by the king. Given this context, we easily can imagine that the wise men's appearance in Jerusalem was not welcomed by Herod, the religious leaders, and Herod's supporters.

On the surface Herod treated the magi with an appropriate level of deference; but their arrival magnified Herod's paranoia. With King Herod and now a "newborn king of the Jews" there are too many kings in this picture. Something had to give.

THE INQUIRING KING

Interestingly, in Matthew 2:4 Herod called together the chief priests and the scribes to ask where the Messiah was to be born. It wasn't evident from the inquiries of the magi that they were talking about the Messiah. They simply had asked about the birth of a royal prince. But in keeping with Matthew's story of Jesus's birth that is focused on establishing Jesus as the Messiah, Herod's immediate interpretation is that the magi were referring to the Messiah. Perhaps the appearance of the star convinced him that this was no ordinary king of the Jews.

The chief priests and scribes loosely cited Micah 5:2 and 2 Samuel 5:2 to support their conclusion that the Messiah was to be born in Bethlehem. The religious scholars therefore, unwittingly, gave their support to Matthew's claim that Jesus was the long-awaited Messiah. If we didn't know anything about Herod's penchant for violence and paranoia, we might want to give him the benefit of the doubt and think that his question to the religious experts was simply seeking information to pass on to the magi. That delusion will soon dissipate.

THE PLOTTING KING

Herod now knew the place of the birth of this king of the Jews; all that remained was to determine when the birth took place. For this information Herod summoned the wise men for a secret conference. Perhaps innocently, the wise men disclosed to Herod the exact time that the star had appeared in the sky. Herod drew the conclusion that the star's appearance coincided with the birth of this royal child. Herod's scheme, however, had another element to it. He sent the magi to Bethlehem to locate the child for him. For Herod or his servants to search Bethlehem would have created awkward questions and may have been met with resistance. So Herod enlisted the assistance of the wise men, instructing them to search thoroughly for the child and then to return to Jerusalem to inform him of the location of the child so that he, too, could go and pay homage to the child.

The stage was now set. Herod's scheme had been put into motion. Everything now hinged upon the wise men and what they would do next.

Chapter 12: Fear and Joy

Matthew 2:1-12

The journey from Jerusalem to Bethlehem is not long—only a matter of a few miles. But that short trek marks a dramatic distance between the wise men and King Herod. The king greeted the birth of the Messiah with fear and paranoia; the magi greeted the child with unbridled joy.

THE WORSHIPPING WISE MEN

Dispatched by King Herod to Bethlehem to gather information about the location of the child king, the wise men found that they actually didn't need his assistance because the star now led them until it stopped over the place where the child was. Matthew tells us that when they arrived, the magi were filled with overwhelming joy (2:10). Then they knelt before the child and paid homage to him. While in the immediate context of this scene in the house in Bethlehem it may be possible to interpret the kneeling and homage of the wise men as simply a matter of showing due respect to a newborn prince, in light of all that Matthew has already asserted about Jesus's identity as the Messiah who was conceived by the

Holy Spirit, we also should regard this as an act of worship. The magi's actions demonstrated their openness to this new act of God—an openness of which Herod was not capable. Their gifts of gold, frankincense and myrrh are extravagant, once again confirming their abundant joy and their worship of the infant Jesus.

Matthew contrasts the response of Herod to the news of Jesus's birth with the response of the wise men. Herod gained and maintained power through subterfuge and violence. His was a kingdom established in the ways of the world. For Herod, power trumped everything and the news of the birth of a new king was received as a threat. Matthew notes the fear that took possession of Herod and all of Jerusalem. The king knew that any weakness, any potential threat could spark an uprising against him.

In this light, it is little wonder that Herod's meeting with the wise men was shrouded in secrecy. Word about the birth of a new king, the Messiah, was like a spark near a powder keg. It would stir up all kinds of hopes and aspirations among Herod's subjects. Unless this spark was doused quickly, Herod's entire kingdom could explode in his face.

A DANGEROUS HOPE

The hope of the Messiah could be a powerful threat because if it took root it could awaken Herod's people to the reality of their lives and more importantly to the hope that their lives could be better. As long as talk of the Messiah focused on the distant future so that it was beyond the reach of mortals, Herod was safe. But a Messiah already born? That posed a clear and present danger.

The real threat to Herod, however, was not military or even political; it was hope. Hope for a future that was fundamentally different from the troubled present under the domination of the

Roman Empire and a Jewish vassal king. Hope that the social, economic, and military domination by Rome and Herod might be coming to an end. Hope for a king who would be just and righteous, compassionate and gracious. Hope for the Messiah.

Herod's real enemy, then, was not a cabal of rebels ready to take up arms against him. Ideas, hopes, and dreams were the real threat. Recognition that another way in the world is possible could stoke more trouble for Herod than any armed revolt that was simply a grab for power. If Herod could crush these hopes, if he could neutralize this Messiah, then he would be safe.

A STRIKING CONTRAST

The contrasting responses of Herod and the wise men initially are surprising for another reason. We might expect Herod, as a Jew, to be receptive to the arrival of the Messiah. But as will happen repeatedly in Matthew, those who should have received Jesus joyfully in fact viewed him with fear, suspicion, and murder in their hearts. They have much to lose they think and cannot respond with joy to the good news of his birth. Too much is at stake. They are too bound to the way things are to be open to how they might be.

But the wise men, foreigners from a distant land, unschooled in the ways and means of Israel's God, prove to be more receptive. They display openness to the good news of the Messiah's birth. Their joy overflows. They kneel before the child, offering their worship and gifts.

A CHOICE TO MAKE

The birth of Jesus confronted Herod and the wise men—and confronts us—with a choice about how we will respond to the good news of Jesus's birth. Will we experience the coming of the

Messiah as good news or as a threat? Will we be able to embrace the child and his kingdom? Or will we cling to our power, our self-determination and our riches, hoarding our paltry treasures, but depriving ourselves of the overwhelming joy that comes to those who kneel before Jesus? The choice is not easy.

Chapter 13: Dreams and Other Instructions

Matthew 2:13-23

I have to admit that I have never had a dream in which an angel appeared to me and told me what to do. So, at one level it is difficult for me to identify with the experience of Joseph. The way the story of Jesus's birth unfolds in Matthew 1-2, it almost seems as though Joseph couldn't get a good night's sleep! In Matthew 1:20-23, when Joseph was considering the possibility of divorcing his pregnant fiancé, an angel of the Lord appeared to him and told him not to do so. Now, in chapter 2 an angel appears to Joseph to warn him of the danger posed by King Herod. Joseph is told to flee to Egypt and wait there for further instructions (2:13). Then in 2:19-20 in yet another dream, an angel instructed Joseph that the danger had passed and it was time to return to the land of Israel. Finally, Joseph was warned to avoid returning to Bethlehem because the danger there still was too great (2:22). So Joseph took his wife and son to Nazareth where they settled down. The repeated interventions by the angel of the Lord with instructions to guide Joseph seems remote to us because they fall outside the experience of most of us.

We should note, however, that the angelic communications do not stand on their own in Matthew. They usually are accompanied by references to the fulfilment of words that were spoken by the prophets. As we have indicated before, Matthew has a habit of linking events in the story of Jesus with texts from the Old Testament and especially from the prophets of ancient Israel. For Matthew, these linkages helped him to make sense of the life of Jesus. They helped to convey his deep conviction, shared with other Christians, that God was at work even in the midst of tragic events such as the killing of infants. The events of Jesus's life are not random, but rather are part of an overarching divine plan for the salvation of the world (Matthew 1:21).

VISIONS IN THE NIGHT

Two further observations seem relevant to these nocturnal revelations. First, I think that it is worth noting that these kinds of nighttime disclosures tend to come in moments of uncertainty. We could recall the nocturnal encounters that Jacob had with God, first when he was fleeing from the murderous anger of his brother Esau (Genesis 28:10-22) and then in his anticipation of a reunion with Esau many years later (Genesis 32:22-32). These two encounters with God came at moments of vulnerability, when Jacob's immediate future seemed to be in danger. His guard was down and his tendency toward self-reliance and self-assertion seemed to have led to a dead end. In the nocturnally blurred lines between reality and vision, Jacob's eyes and ears were opened. In the case of Joseph, the danger posed by Herod's treacherous scheme required an extraordinary intervention by God. A clear and present danger rendered Joseph receptive to the dream. His guard was down and he could now hear the angel of the Lord.

Second, I think that we should recall that Joseph was described earlier as "a righteous man" (Matthew 1:19). This is not just a throwaway comment. Joseph, as a righteous person, developed deep habits of prayer and worship that would have placed him in a position to receive these night messages from God. His disciplines of the spirit made him receptive to God's leading. His ears could hear clearly and his eyes could see clearly what the messages from God were saying to him. His heart was open and responsive. In other words, Joseph had developed habits that placed him in a space where God could speak and Joseph could listen.

DECLUTTERING

These two observations suggest that fundamental to Joseph's ability to hear the word of the Lord spoken through the angel was his focused, uncluttered heart and mind. In a crisis our attention narrows; extraneous events and concerns recede into the background. So, for example, when we face a significant life crisis such as a serious illness, things that once dominated our attention fall away as survival becomes our focus. The clutter of "things" melts away as we focus on what really matters. We see more clearly what we value in life and we hear more clearly those voices that have been muted for too long. It is no accident that life transitions often stir in people a need for the security of religion as we seek to restore the familiar equilibrium that has made life liveable. In the case of Joseph, the imminent danger posed by Herod's treachery coupled with his own disciplines of listening sharpened his attentiveness to God.

Part of the observance of Advent is the practice of peeling away some of the extraneous trappings of our life to enable us to receive once again the child of Bethlehem. Of course, this is easier said than done in our commercial observance of Christmas when we are run off our feet with all the distractions of gift-giving and parties. Yet, if we are to hear the angels or to receive the Word of the Lord, it is precisely this discipline of listening that we must hone. Who knows, we might even hear an angel speak to us in a dream.

Chapter 14: Refugees

Matthew 2:13-23

The most current available information estimates that there are almost 68 million refugees in the world. The number is staggering. People on the move, fleeing from many forms of oppression and violence, search desperately for safety. Sometimes they are welcomed; but in recent years we have seen refugees characterized as "illegal aliens," "outsiders," and "rapists" and their search for safety has been described as an "invasion" and an "infestation." Suspicion and resistance to the acceptance of refugees in some countries and regions seems to be growing. Displaced persons have few rights and little leverage to advocate for themselves. When they cross national boundaries in their search for a safe place, as non-citizens in a foreign land they are vulnerable.

For those of us who are privileged to live in safety and security, it is perhaps surprising to think of Joseph, Mary, and Jesus as refugees. Yet when we read this passage closely, we come to the realization that this was exactly their experience. Their story can help us to put a human face on the plight of modern-day displaced persons.

HEROD'S MURDEROUS PLAN

King Herod was notorious for his ruthlessness. He was a tyrannical monarch who would use every means available to cling to power. He had close members of his family murdered because he suspected them of plotting against him. Any hint of threat would prompt a spasm of violence. So, when the wise men arrived in Jerusalem searching for a newborn king of the Jews, what Herod heard was not good news but rather a threat to his rule. We should not be surprised that Herod was moved to duplicity and violence.

The duplicity of Herod was evident in his instructions to the magi. He wanted them to search for the child and then to report back to him so that he, in turn, could pay homage to this infant king of the Jews. But, of course, this was a ruse. Herod's real intent was to gain valuable information that would afford him the opportunity to eliminate the threat. When Herod finally clued in to the fact that he himself had been duped by the wise men who returned home by another route rather than coming back to Jerusalem, he set in motion a typically Herodian strategy: kill all the infants in Bethlehem who were two years old and younger. Given the estimated population of Bethlehem at the time, this probably meant that no more than twenty children were at risk. But among them would have been the infant Jesus.

After a warning from the angel of the Lord, Joseph escaped in the night with Mary and Jesus to seek safety in Egypt. Jews had used Egypt as a safe haven a number of times in the past. Abraham and Sarah had fled to Egypt to escape a famine (Genesis 12:10-20); Joseph's brothers traveled to Egypt to find food (Genesis 42);

Jeroboam had escaped to Egypt to avoid the consequences of his rebellion against King Solomon (1 Kings 11:40); and a number of Jews, including the prophet Jeremiah, settled in Egypt after the Babylonian defeat of Judah in 586 BCE. Yet we shouldn't think that Egypt was always a hospitable host to these displaced persons. After all, the Egyptian king took Sarah into his harem when she and Abraham crossed into Egypt. Later, the enslavement of the Hebrews and the entire exodus story grew out of the settlement of Joseph and his family in Egypt as refugees. It's clear from reading the book of Exodus that even after several generations the Hebrews were viewed as outsiders by the Egyptians and became increasingly vulnerable as aliens in a foreign land.

Now it was Joseph, Mary, and Jesus who sought refuge in Egypt. They were vulnerable, without legal status, and frightened. Matthew doesn't dwell on the details of their status and vulnerability; his readers immediately would have recognized the defencelessness of the holy family. Matthew's reticence about amplifying this experience should not cause us to lose sight of the fact that Jesus himself had been a refugee with all that flows from this status!

REFUGEES – "THE LEAST OF THESE"

When I think about it, the fact that Matthew records this refugee experience of Jesus—even as a young child—throws into a new light Jesus's later discourse about the judgment when the Son of Man will separate the sheep from the goats. "Then the king will say to those at his right hand, 'Come, you that are blessed by my Father, inherit the kingdom prepared for you from the foundation of the world; for I was hungry and you gave me food, I was thirsty and you gave me something to drink, I was a stranger and you welcomed me, I was naked and you gave me clothing, I was sick and you took care of me, I was in prison and you visited me'" (Matthew 25:34-36). As the scene develops the righteous question the judge, "'Lord, when was it that we saw you hungry and gave you food, or thirsty and gave you something to drink? And when was it that we saw you a stranger and welcomed you, or naked and gave you clothing? And when was it that we saw you sick or in prison and visited you?'" (Matthew 25:37-39). The response of the king encapsulates the essence of the narrative: "Truly I tell you, just as you did it to one of the least of these who are members of my family, you did it to me" (Matthew 25:40).

The flight of Joseph and his family from the treachery of Herod and their refugee experience in Egypt surely qualified them as being among "the least of these." This story reminds us that the good news is not only for the affluent and the comfortable, but most especially is for the least—those who are vulnerable, discarded, and displaced. Right from the beginning of the story of Jesus Matthew claims that the gospel is good news and that we, if we are to live in harmony with the mission of Jesus, are to care for those who are most vulnerable and especially for the refugees of our world. Who knows, we may even be caring for Jesus incognito.

Chapter 15: Déjà vu

Matthew 2:13-23

The exodus of the Hebrew slaves from their bondage in Egypt was the foundational story that held the people of Israel together. The experience of bitter slavery, the astonishing intervention of the LORD to deliver them out of Egypt, and the dramatic crossing of the Red Sea shaped the identity of the Jewish people throughout their history. The annual observance of Passover, celebrating the escape from Egypt, provided a touchstone for Israel.

It is little wonder then, that centuries later, when the Jews were in exile in Babylon, the great prophet of the exile, known to scholars as "Second Isaiah" (Isaiah 40-55), reached back to the exodus to anticipate the LORD's new deliverance of God's people from their distress. Isaiah 40-55 is filled with images drawn from Exodus. The LORD will lead his people from Babylon, through the wilderness, to their homeland with a mighty hand and an outstretched arm. While this is a new act of God on behalf of Israel, it is patterned after the prior experience of deliverance from the horrors of Egyptian slavery.

A NEW EXODUS

We should not be surprised, then, that in telling his story of Jesus, Matthew should reach back to the very beginning of Israel's history as a people. The lens through which Matthew would have us read the story of Jesus's birth marks this as another "exodus"; another act of divine deliverance. The message is clear: the coming of Jesus takes its place in the succession of the saving acts of God stretching all the way back to Israel's earliest days.

The similarities between the exodus story and the story of the holy family's sojourn in Egypt are striking. First of all, in both narratives, the oppression is initiated by a king out of frantic fear. In the exodus story the culprit is the Egyptian Pharaoh who stirs up the irrational fears of his people to enlist their support for his genocidal plot to kill Hebrew infant boys (Exodus 1); in Matthew the villain is King Herod who, fearful of the birth of a new "king of the Jews," perceives a threat to his own position and initiates his own murderous attack on infants. Both in Exodus and in Matthew we find that the oppressor king institutes a policy of infanticide, trying to eliminate any perceived threat by the murder of infants.

While in the exodus story Egypt is the place of oppression and the Israelites escape to the wilderness and ultimately to the promised land, in Matthew the initial movement of Mary, Joseph, and Jesus is in the opposite direction. The holy family escapes *to* Egypt from the threat posed by Herod.

In Exodus the return of Moses to Egypt to undertake his mission to deliver Israel from their oppression is prompted by the death of the Pharaoh; in Matthew the death of King Herod prompts the return of Joseph, Mary, and Jesus to the land of Israel.

Matthew makes the connection between the exodus narrative and the story of Jesus explicit in verse 15 with his citation from Hosea 11:1, "This was to fulfill what had been spoken by the Lord through the prophet, 'Out of Egypt I have called my son.'" Just as God had called his son, Israel, out of Egypt at the time of the exodus, so now God calls his son, Jesus, out of Egypt. The connection is unmistakeable.

DELIVERANCE FROM OPPRESSORS

Putting this all together, we can see that Matthew teaches us that God has worked consistently to deliver people from their oppressors. In some cases these oppressors are real people—that is, they are kings and leaders who prey on the fears of their followers to stir them to acts of violence against identifiable groups. In other cases the "oppressors" are more metaphorical, but no less real—our sins and obsessions that enslave us and drive us to destructive actions and attitudes. They are the distortions that separate us from our neighbours and from God. Yet, throughout the biblical story God strives to overcome these oppressors. God protects his people; God prepares a way through the wilderness to safety. God saves his people! And now, with the coming of Jesus, Matthew teaches us that God acts definitively, in a new way, to deliver us. So while the birth of Jesus follows in the long line of God's saving acts, it is more than that. The birth of Jesus runs into many of the same oppressive tyrants as God's previous efforts to deliver; but according to Matthew Jesus fulfills God's plan. His coming marks a turning point, a decisive initiative, a new way. As we learn a little later in Matthew, the birth of Jesus marks the coming of the kingdom of heaven.

What Matthew teaches us, therefore, is that there is a striking persistence to God's determination to save the world from the powerful, oppressive effects of sin and its agents. Generation after generation of Israelites retold the story of these efforts. But now God sends his Son, our Lord Jesus Christ, first as a newborn, weak and vulnerable. Soon, however, we will encounter Jesus as a teacher, prophet and saviour.

Matthew's story of the birth of Jesus is only the beginning. But in his telling of this story, Matthew sets the groundwork for the story that will unfold in the rest of his Gospel. The rejoicing of the wise men will be taken up by those who heed the call of Jesus to follow him.

PART TWO: PREPARATION FOR JESUS'S MINISTRY

Chapter 16: John the Baptist

Matthew 3:1-12

H aving laid the groundwork for the story of Jesus in chapters 1 and 2, Matthew next moves us closer to the launch of Jesus's public ministry. The Evangelist sets the story of Jesus within the larger context of the biblical narrative through his portrayal of the ministry of John the Baptist. Unlike the Gospel of Luke's account in which Luke provides a detailed introduction to the birth of John and a familial connection with Jesus, Matthew's introduction of John comes out of the blue. Matthew does not mention any previous relationship between Jesus and John; from reading Matthew alone one might draw the conclusion that Jesus and John had no previous connection whatsoever. For Matthew, the Baptist's significance is grounded in the larger work of God rather than in any other relationship.

A PROPHET APPEARS

Matthew's description of John the Baptist provides details that convey the significance of John's arrival in the wilderness near the Jordan River. First of all, John's clothing (camel hair garments with a leather belt) and his diet (locusts and wild honey) mark him as one who leads a subsistence-level life. But more importantly for Matthew these details identify John as a prophet (see 2 Kings 1:8; Zechariah 13:4). Second, John delivers a message focused on repentance, judgment and the approach of the kingdom of heaven. The details of John's appearance, his diet and his message all point to the specific identification of John as a prophet. That is, John the Baptist stands within the tradition of the Old Testament prophets.

Matthew, however, further interprets John's activity within the larger work of God by citing Isaiah 40:3 and observing that John fulfills this prophetic and preparatory role. John the Baptist is the one who prepares the way for the coming of God in Jesus (see also Malachi 3:1).

A PROPHET LIKE ELIJAH

In some Jewish traditions, this preparatory role is associated with the great Israelite prophet Elijah. As Matthew presents it, this is an identification that Jesus himself acknowledges later in the gospel. In Matthew 11:7-19 Jesus praises John and explicitly associates him with the great prophet Elijah. Further, in Matthew 17:9-13 Jesus discusses with his disciples the tradition that maintained that prior to the coming of the Son of Man Elijah would return to prepare the way. Then, in an editorial comment, Matthew states that the disciples interpreted Jesus's words to be referring to John the Baptist. That is, John the Baptist is the Elijah-like figure who must come before the arrival of the Messiah.

Therefore, while in Matthew 3:1-12 the Evangelist is restrained and subtle in his identification of John the Baptist with the prophet Elijah, it is evident that as his story of Jesus progresses, Matthew wants to make clear to his readers precisely the significance of John's appearance: as the Elijah-like figure, John prepares the way for the coming of Jesus. The appearance of John the Baptist is not a coincidence; it is not random. It is, rather, part of the unfolding plan of God, foretold by the prophets and confirmed by the details provided in Matthew's three descriptions of John and his mission. The arrival of John the Baptist signals the coming of God's agent of salvation. Thus the real intent of the inclusion of the narratives about John the Baptist is to provide further confirmation for Matthew's overarching claim that Jesus is the Messiah, the son of David, the son of Abraham, and the son of God.

THE ONE WHO PREPARES THE WAY

Despite the importance of John the Baptist in the plan of God as the one who prepares the way for the Messiah, Matthew makes clear that John himself never is the focus of the Gospel. In Matthew 3:11-12 the gospel-writer quotes John as placing himself in a secondary role to the one who will come after him. Matthew accomplishes this in two ways. First, John establishes a contrast between the baptism with water that he practices and the baptism with the Holy Spirit and fire that Jesus will bring. Second, John asserts that the imbalance in importance and power between the two of them is so overwhelming that he is not worthy even to carry the sandals of Jesus—a task so menial that it would be assigned only to the lowest of slaves. John the Baptist has a role to play in salvation history, but it is limited and it is subordinate to that of Jesus who will "save his people from their sins" (Matthew 1:21).

Historians hypothesize that John the Baptist was an important figure in early first-century Judaism. Even the Jewish historian Josephus makes reference to John and his disciples. Some scholars even speculate that the movement established by John the Baptist may have rivalled the earliest Christian movement in importance. But Matthew, along with the other New Testament gospel-writers, clearly subordinates the Baptist to Jesus. There is no contest between them in terms of importance. John's role is preparatory; Jesus is the real thing!

Matthew keeps hammering home the central concern of these early chapters of his Gospel: the identity and mission of Jesus as the Messiah. He seemingly never tires of presenting his argument from a new angle. In this passage, the appearance of John the Baptist is seen as the fulfillment of the necessary preparatory work before Jesus can begin his public ministry. According to Matthew, all this takes place in accordance with the Scriptures. According to Matthew this is God's plan.

Chapter 17: Repent!

Matthew 3:1-12

The basic message of John the Baptist was astonishingly simple: "Repent, for the kingdom of heaven has come near" (Matthew 3:2). Three components make up this simple statement. First, there is a call to repentance. Second there is reference to the kingdom of heaven. Third there is the claim that the kingdom of heaven has come near. To unpack John's statement it is necessary in this study and the next to consider all three parts.

CHANGING DIRECTION

Typical of the prophet that he was, John the Baptist called upon his audience to "repent." In common English "repent" often means simply to say we're sorry for something. It is taken to mean little more than to express regret. But while regret for some action may be a component of repentance, it is far from the central point. The New Testament Greek term *metanoia* that is usually translated as repentance suggests a much deeper response. Its Hebrew counterpart, *šûb*, means to turn around, change direction, and more metaphorically is used to represent a radical reorientation of life. That connotation of radical change of direction deeply influenced the use of the Greek term *metanoia* in the New Testament and in John's proclamation.

In the light of these observations, John's summons to repentance represented far more than saying we're sorry; it called for a radical turning, a transformation, leaving behind an old way of life and embarking upon a new path. The old ways must be put aside; a new way of life must be undertaken. Repentance implies a thorough conversion.

REPENTANCE TAKES TIME

In the revivalist tradition of Christianity we have come to think of repentance as an instantaneous act that brings with it an instantaneous conversion from an old life to a new life. While in theory it may be the case that such rapid, thoroughgoing conversions are possible, in practice conversion is a much longer and more complex process than this. Repentance is not a momentary emotional response and conversion is not an instantaneous change.

Sometimes repentance can be superficial and momentary. For example, the prophet Hosea exposed the superficiality of Israel's repentance in Hosea 6:1-3. In response to the prophet's preaching and the disasters that had befallen them, the Israelites repeated a liturgy of repentance. "Come, let us return to the LORD; for it is he who has torn, and he will heal us; he has struck down, and he will bind us up...Let us know, let us press on to know the LORD..." The repentance (that is, the desire to return to the LORD) seemed to be in order; it sounded sincere. All the right words were spoken. But in Hosea 6:4 the voice of God announced that Israel's devotion and repentance were like a morning fog that dissipates when the sun appears or like the summer dew on the grass that evaporates with the first rays of the sun. Repentance that is this transitory is no repentance at all.

The problem is that thinking of repentance as a quick fix reflects a superficial understanding of the nature and imprint of sin upon our lives. Sin is not only wilful acts of wrongdoing which we can abandon if only our determination is strong enough. Sin runs deep within us. Its marks are found not just on the surface level of our actions, but in our dispositions, in our heart. Sin shapes our character, warps our hearts and minds, and draws us in harmful directions. The distortions of sin penetrate deep into us.

It is for this reason that in the Sermon on the Mount (Matthew 5-7) Jesus spoke of a greater righteousness that penetrates beneath the surface of our lives to impact our hearts as the centre of our existence. The transformation of which both John the Baptist and Jesus spoke is one which transforms from the inside out.

FRUIT WORTHY OF REPENTANCE

More often than not, repentance and conversion, if they are to address the depths of human depravity, require time and effort—as well as an abundance of God's grace. Repentance and conversion are not one-time, instantaneous accomplishments. Rather, they are long-term, often painful processes. It is for this reason that a few verses later in the account of his preaching, John warned the Pharisees and Sadducees to "bear fruit worthy of repentance" (Matthew 3:8). It takes time for trees to bear fruit; it also takes time for repentance to produce the kind of conversion of which John spoke. And in Matthew's story of Jesus, trees that don't bear fruit wither and die (Matthew 21:18-22).

John the Baptist summoned his listeners to a repentance that had substance. He called for repentance that actually produced results. He called for a true conversion that runs deep into those who respond—a conversion the depth of which matches the depth of the imprint of sin itself upon our lives. This is no easy conversion; it is possible only by the grace of God.

Chapter 18: The Kingdom Has Come Near

Matthew 3:1-12

We have already thought about John the Baptist's call to repentance. Now we move on to consider the rationale for this summons. As Matthew reports it, John's proclamation is: "Repent, for the kingdom of heaven has come near." The key word here is "for." It could be translated as "because" giving us the slightly different reading, "Repent, *because* the kingdom of heaven has come near."[1]

---

[1] Matthew typically uses the expression "kingdom of heaven" rather than "kingdom of God" that is found in Mark and Luke. Many reasons have been given for this difference in terminology, but the fundamental meaning is the same whether the gospel-writers refer to the kingdom of heaven or the kingdom of God.

THE APPROACH OF THE KINGDOM

The basis of John's message of repentance is the claim that the kingdom of heaven "has come near." The Greek term translated in the NRSV as "has come near" has been rendered in a number of other ways. Some translate it to mean that the kingdom "has arrived"; others render it as the kingdom "has come"; or still others, the kingdom "is here." What all of these translations attempt to express is the assertion of John (and later of Jesus) that the kingdom of heaven is no longer a distant prospect in a faraway future; rather, the kingdom of heaven is right in front of us; it is here now, at least in some sense. For John the Baptist, in his context, the proclamation that the kingdom of heaven was imminent marked an important turning point. With the impending commencement of Jesus's ministry, history was about to take a dramatic turn. The importance of the approach of the kingdom of heaven and the consequent summons to repentance is confirmed by the fact that in Matthew 4:17 Jesus's first pronouncement is said to have been exactly the same announcement of the arrival of the kingdom. A little later in Matthew (10:7) the disciples of Jesus were instructed to make the proclamation of the arrival of the kingdom of heaven their central message.

THE URGENCY OF THE KINGDOM

The arrival of the kingdom of heaven creates urgency. Things are about to change. This change is so substantial that it requires some kind of response. It's a game-changer. According to John, the appropriate response is repentance, a reorientation of life. Because the kingdom has come near, repentance must be our response.

Of course, the obvious question that arises from this is, "Why is the arrival of the kingdom of heaven so important?" The kingdom of heaven refers to the determination of God to establish his just rule in the world. When the kingdom of heaven comes, the injustices and unrighteousness of the world will be overcome by the rule of God. The mighty shall be overthrown and the weak shall be lifted up. God's will shall be done.

JESUS BRINGS THE KINGDOM

What prompts John's announcement that the kingdom of heaven has come near? We should not be surprised to learn that according to Matthew the decisive turning-point is the arrival of Jesus. From the beginning of his account of the life of Jesus, Matthew has been making his point that the coming of Jesus has significance on many levels. This significance has been suggested with the lengthy genealogy that traces Jesus's ancestry to father Abraham; it has been indicated by the appearance of angels and stars; it has been made explicit by the astonishing birth of Jesus to the virgin Mary and his designation as the son of Joseph and the son of God; it has been asserted by the assignment of Jesus's name because "he will save his people from their sins"; it has been affirmed by the arrival of the wise men from the east; and now the imminent appearance of Jesus on the public scene prompts John's announcement that the kingdom of heaven has come near. In all these ways, Matthew has been leading us to this climactic assertion.

A CONTESTED KINGDOM

Yet if we read further in Matthew's gospel we find that the arrival of the kingdom of heaven is contested. That is, not everyone accepts this claim. There are those who challenge John's claim. There will be those who contest Jesus's preaching, who refuse to accept his place in the larger story. Just as King Herod had responded with fear and then violence to the news that the wise men brought to him, so too there will be others in Matthew's account who respond to Jesus himself with fear and then violence. The coming of the kingdom of heaven is not all rose petals; it also brings thorns with it.

The nature of the kingdom of heaven will be explored throughout Matthew as Jesus teaches his disciples what it is all about. In the Sermon on the Mount (Matthew 5-7) Jesus provides instruction about the qualities that will be characteristic of the community that is grounded in the good news of the arrival of the kingdom of heaven. Through a series of parables in Matthew 13 Jesus instructs his disciples about the nature of the kingdom. And through the predictions of his own suffering, Jesus recasts the nature of the kingdom of heaven in light of his own journey toward Jerusalem.

John's fundamental assertion is that the kingdom of heaven has come near; it is no longer on the distant horizon but rather is right in front of us. The gateway into the kingdom of heaven is repentance. It is the only gateway because the coming of the kingdom of heaven requires a complete reorientation of life.

Chapter 19: The Pharisees and Sadducees Among Us

Matthew 3:1-12

The response to the preaching of John the Baptist was impressive. As Matthew describes it, people from Jerusalem, Judaea and the area around the Jordan River flocked to hear him. But more than hearing him, the people were being baptized in the Jordan and confessing their sins. With his preaching and the response of the people, John truly was preparing the way for the Lord as Matthew asserted in verse 3, with his citation from Isaiah 40:3. But there was a complication.

SCOUTING OUT THE OPPOSITION?

According to Matthew, among those who came to John for baptism were many Pharisees and Sadducees. This is their first appearance in Matthew, so we should take a moment to introduce them. Scholars sometimes express some surprise that the Pharisees and Sadducees are lumped together here because in many ways they were rivals in the Judaism of the first century. The Pharisees had a deep concern for the proper observance of God's will as expressed in the Law or the Torah. They were keenly observant Jews. The Sadducees were aligned more with the religious centre of power and the Roman establishment in Jerusalem. Frequently they would make religious and political compromises that the Pharisees found offensive.

The presence of the Pharisees and Sadducees among those who went out to find John the Baptist is surprising. John's message of the imminent kingdom of heaven and the call to repentance would have been suspicious, implying as it would that the official practice of Judaism was falling short. Typical of religious figures who are part of the establishment, the Pharisees and Sadducees would have been concerned with any movement that could undermine or delegitimize their own religious practice and power. Some suggest that these religious leaders were on a spying mission, trying to find out exactly what was going on in the wilderness near the Jordan River. What was all the fuss about?

Whatever the reason for the presence of the Pharisees and Sadducees among the crowd around John the Baptist, his response to them was sharply critical. John called them a "brood of vipers," surely a provocative and confrontational label. But John was just getting warmed up. He implicitly criticized them for a false repentance, one that did not produce the proper fruit (verse 8). Then, even more provocatively, John warned them to avoid reliance upon their pedigree as descendants of Abraham. This Abrahamic heritage was not enough to spare them from the impending judgment. After all, could not God raise up descendants of Abraham from the rocks lying on the ground? More than ancestry was needed!

JUDGMENT IS COMING

The presence of Sadducees and Pharisees led John the Baptist to focus on the impending judgment that would come with the arrival of the kingdom of heaven. We tend to think of judgment in terms of punishment. While some of the content of these verses fits with this interpretation, it seems to me that the text also thinks of judgment in terms of discernment or sorting out. If among those who came to John the Baptist for baptism there were both some who came with sincere hearts confessing their sins and some others who came for less praiseworthy reasons, this judgment would sort that out. That's the force of John's metaphor of the threshing floor and the separation of wheat from chaff in verse 12. It is also the message of Jesus's parable of the wheat and weeds in Matthew 13:24-30 and its interpretation in 13:36-43. In this parable, the kingdom of heaven is like a field in which wheat and weeds grow up together to be separated only at the harvest. At that time the weeds will be gathered together and burned.

If in Jesus's parable concerning the kingdom of heaven the wheat and the weeds are permitted to sprout and mature side-by-side, this may help us to understand the presence of the Pharisees and Sadducees among the pious people who have streamed into the wilderness to hear John the Baptist. John's warnings to these "weeds" notwithstanding, their presence will be resolved in the judgment that is coming with the kingdom of heaven. They are being properly warned by John about the judgment that they will face. But in the meantime, they will sprout and grow alongside the sincere and productive followers of John (and ultimately of Jesus). Those who produce fruit consistent with repentance (Matthew 3:8) will be the wheat; those who do not will be like a barren fruit tree that is cut down (Matthew 3:10) and burned or like the chaff that will be gathered and burned (Matthew 3:12). Sorting out the truly penitent from the superficially penitent is the work of God in judgment in the kingdom of heaven.

THE WEEDS AMONG US

It's important for us not to think of the Pharisees and Sadducees simply as the Jews who opposed John the Baptist and, later in Matthew, Jesus. Pharisees and Sadducees come in many shapes and forms. There are Christian "Pharisees" and Christian "Sadducees" all around us and among us—those who outwardly appear to be sincere, going through all the motions of religiosity but who on the inside are devoid of the repentance to which both John and Jesus summoned their true followers. It's not our job to weed them out; we need to leave that task to God when the kingdom of heaven comes in its fullness.

Chapter 20: A Surprising Baptism

Matthew 3:13-17

Baptism played an important role in the ministry of John the Baptist. It is mentioned first in Matthew 3:6-7 in the description of the response to the preaching of John. As Matthew describes it, crowds descended upon the Jordan River in order to be baptized. The baptism practised by John was associated with repentance and the confession of sins. A few verses later (verses 11-12) John contrasts the baptism that he administers with that which will be practised by the one who is to come after him. In this comparison, John's baptism with water for repentance pales next to the anticipated baptism with the Holy Spirit and fire. The surprising thing about the verses we are considering now is that Jesus approaches John the Baptist and requests that John baptize him.

A DIFFERENT APPROACH

However, before we consider Jesus's request and its significance we need to recognize that Matthew establishes a contrast between the approach of the Pharisees and Sadducees for baptism and the approach of Jesus. John recognizes and calls out the religious leaders, chastising them for their lack of fruit worthy of repentance (verse 8). For them baptism for repentance is useless without accompanying evidence of repentance. Baptism holds no inherent power without commitment to change. John's objection to baptizing the religious leaders leads to a warning that judgment is near and that they had better produce the required fruit of repentance.

In contrast, John objects to the request of Jesus to be baptized because he (that is, John) is not worthy to baptize Jesus. Having in the previous verses spoken about the one who would come after him and his own unworthiness in comparison with that one, John now objects to Jesus's request for baptism because it is Jesus who should be baptizing John! The contrast between John's response to these two requests for baptism could not be more sharp.

One of the questions that troubles scholars is, Why would Jesus make a request to be baptized by John? After all, if John's baptism is for the forgiveness of sins and, as later Christian teaching insists, Jesus is without sin (see Hebrews 4:15), then Jesus is not in need of forgiveness. In the case of Jesus, baptism is completely unnecessary and perhaps easily misunderstood.

As we have noted, John's own reason for objecting to Jesus's request initially appears to be more about the relative unworthiness of John to even carry Jesus's sandals, let alone baptize him (Matthew 3:11). John needs to be baptized by Jesus rather than the other way around. The Baptist knows his place when in the presence of Jesus.

FULFILLING ALL RIGHTEOUSNESS

Yet in this scene Jesus insists that John baptize him in order to "fulfill all righteousness" (Matthew 3:15). But what does this mean? Commentators have suggested several ways to understand this statement. First, some argue that with his baptism Jesus is cementing his identification with his people. Jesus comes not as one who is above or over those who follow him. He does not come as someone who remains segregated from the masses. In his humility, Jesus becomes one of the people in significant ways. After all, earlier in Matthew one of the names given to Jesus is Immanuel, God is with us.

Second, for others "fulfilling all righteousness" refers to following the path set out by God for the salvation of the world. In the plan of God John's role is to be the one who prepares the way for the coming of the Messiah; that preparation includes this scene and what will follow immediately in the next verses. Fulfilling all righteousness is submitting himself to the wishes of Jesus even though it might not be reasonable from John's own perspective. For Jesus, fulfilling all righteousness refers to obedience to his heavenly Father. His submission to baptism is an act of obedience to the will of God.

Finally, righteousness is an important concern in Matthew. The word occurs seven times in the Gospel (3:15; 5:6, 10, 20; 6:1, 33; 21:32). When these occurrences are studied carefully we can see that righteousness in Matthew refers to cultivating the proper relationship with God in both words and actions, both internally and externally. In some circumstances this means obedience to the will of God. But overall, it refers to congruence with the purposes of God; it is an orientation toward God and the kingdom of heaven. Such an orientation shapes life and gives it direction.

Summarizing these various suggestions, Jesus encourages John to baptize him in order to fulfill his mission in obedience to the will of God. With his baptism Jesus signals the orientation of his life toward God. His prime concern is the kingdom of heaven and its coming. He has come to be "God with us" and identifies with us even in baptism. The concern of Jesus to fulfill all righteousness will be tested severely in Matthew 4. But before that, there is one more component in this scene that must be explored.

Chapter 21: A Compelling Revelation

Matthew 3:16-17

As soon as Jesus in baptized by John the Baptist we are ushered into a visionary experience and testimony that forms the climax of Matthew's presentation of Jesus to this point in the Gospel. The scene in these two verses contains three separate elements: the opening of the heavens, the descent of the Spirit, and the divine pronouncement.

A DIVINE AFFIRMATION

It is important to notice that in Matthew's telling of the story, this is an experience to which only Jesus had access; it was not a public event in the sense that those around Jesus at the time would have seen the heavens opened, watched the Spirit descend or heard the voice from heaven. Matthew is quite intentional with his statement that [only] *Jesus* saw the heavens opened and the Spirit descend (verse 16). But Matthew tells this story also for the benefit of his readers, so that we might understand the claim he makes about Jesus. Matthew presents this scene as evidence of the true character of Jesus.

The opening of the heavens was, within the context of early Judaism of the time of Jesus, a way of representing the beginning of the time of God's intervention in the affairs of the world in order to establish God's rule or kingdom. This is consistent with the previous proclamation of John the Baptist that the kingdom of heaven is now present.

Next, we should note that the coming of the Spirit of God upon an individual was associated with the commissioning of various leaders in the history of Israel such as judges, prophets and kings. It was the presence of the Spirit with these persons that validated their place and mission. Especially in Isaiah 61:1 the coming of the Spirit of God upon the servant of God was understood as a decisive marker of the beginning of the rule of God. Thus the descent of the Spirit upon Jesus is a clear sign that he is God's servant.

Finally, the voice from heaven is important because God articulates clearly and forcefully the true identity of Jesus as God's Son and grants God's own stamp of approval. Jesus's designation as the Son of God echoes Psalm 2:7 with its affirmation of the divine sonship of the Messiah. This divine voice affirms that Jesus is the one of whom David spoke; he is the Messiah.

THREE KINDS OF TESTIMONY

When we put this brief episode into the larger context of Matthew's writing we can see that it provides a climactic summary of all that Matthew has said about the identity of Jesus to this point in the Gospel. In these first three chapters (and continuing through the rest of the Gospel), Matthew has drawn upon three different kinds of testimony to confirm his claims about Jesus.

First of all, as we have noted on several occasions, Matthew cites a number of texts from the prophets to interpret the meaning of events in the life of Jesus. According to Matthew Jesus's mission unfolds according to a divine plan. Jesus is not some random individual and the events that have been recounted in Matthew 1-3 are not themselves random. Instead, through the frequent citation of the prophets, Matthew claims that the significance of Jesus can only be discerned when one understands that his coming is part of God's ongoing plan that was revealed through the prophets.

The second witness to the identity of Jesus is the testimony of the prophet in the wilderness, John the Baptist. As Matthew presents him, John is significant only to the extent that he points beyond himself to Jesus. It is John's *testimony* that is significant, not John himself. John's claim is that the arrival of Jesus marks the coming of the kingdom of heaven.

Finally, and most compellingly for Matthew, the voice from heaven—understood to be God's own voice—affirms that Jesus is God's Son. There can be no greater witness to this claim. Everything in Matthew up to this point leads to this affirmation. This is the point that Matthew wants his readers to understand before he launches into the larger narrative about the life, teaching and mission of Jesus. This is the lens through which to see clearly the significance of the story of Jesus.

DISPUTED CLAIMS

As Matthew continues his account of Jesus's life and ministry, we find that his claims about Jesus will be contested. There will be challenges to Jesus's identity, mission and authority. The legitimacy of Jesus's messiahship will be rejected by many. But over and over again Matthew presents his case for the identity of Jesus. Thus, at the moment of Jesus's transfiguration, once again the voice of God affirms Jesus's divine sonship (Matthew 17:5). Finally, at the crucifixion, the Roman centurion's exclamation that "Truly this man was God's Son" stands as a powerful interpretive statement (Matthew 27:54).

According to Matthew, understanding the identity of Jesus is critical to understanding his significance. Jesus is more than a good teacher, a moral philosopher, or an effective orator. None of these are bad things. But they all fall short of Matthew's confession about Jesus. The centurion at the crucifixion summarizes the entire message of Matthew with his confession of Jesus's divine sonship. Within the context of his Gospel, the conflict over the true identity of Jesus comes to a conclusion for Matthew in the death scene of Jesus. But for us the controversy over Jesus's identity is ongoing. For each generation must assess anew its response to Matthew's story. Who is Jesus? That's a question we each must answer.

Chapter 22: The Spirit and the Devil

Matthew 4:1-11

T he baptism of Jesus and the revelation to Jesus by the voice from heaven are followed immediately by a surprising statement: "Then Jesus was *led by the Spirit* into the wilderness to be tempted by the devil" (Matthew 4:1; emphasis added). No sooner had Jesus received the divine confirmation of his identity as God's Son and received the Spirit of God than he was delivered by that same Spirit into the hands of the devil in order to be tested.   Several components of this first verse require exploration.

TEMPTATION OR TEST?

First of all, the NRSV translates the Greek word *peirasthēnai* as "to be tempted." This is a frequent translation of the Greek term. However, this word can also be translated as "to be tested" in the sense of being put to a test. The nuance of these two translations is important. If we follow the translation of the NRSV then the scene that follows will be interpreted as a series of temptations to sin. Jesus is placed in the position of having to resist the enticement to some kind of sinful action. Surely there may be some room for this interpretation in the story. After all, the third temptation to worship the devil rather than God obviously is an enticement to sin. But then we are left with a dilemma: Why would the Spirit of God lead Jesus to be *tempted* by the devil? Would this not be counterproductive?

Personally I find it much more helpful to follow the lead of many commentators who translate the Greek word to mean that Jesus was being "tested." Testing in this case involves a process of discernment and discovery of the true character of Jesus and his mission. The Spirit, in this interpretation, leads Jesus into the wilderness to test the mettle of Jesus. The devil places before Jesus the option of choosing his own mission, defining its character and how he will fulfill it rather than following the path set before him by his heavenly Father. Jesus is being tested to determine the extent to which he will use his status as Son of God for his own benefit. Before the public ministry of Jesus can begin, it is important for Jesus to demonstrate that he understands the character of his mission as God's Son. This requires testing.

GOD TESTS ISRAEL

We might find the idea that God puts people to the test unsettling. But the Old Testament did not. Thus in Genesis 22:1 we read that God tested Abraham by commanding him to sacrifice Isaac. This was an extreme test. After Abraham had chosen to obey the outrageous command of God, the angel of the LORD said to Abraham, "...*now I know* that you fear God..." (Genesis 22:12; emphasis added). The testing of Abraham demonstrated the extreme level of Abraham's willingness to obey the command of God. In addition to the story of Abraham, we also find that God tested Israel on several occasions (Exodus 16:4; 20:20; Deuteronomy 8:2). For example, in the immediate aftermath of the crossing of the Red Sea, the Israelites were faced with a shortage of food. In response, God would provide manna, but with strict instructions for its gathering and distribution. According to Exodus 16:4, these instructions were to "*test them*, whether they will follow my instructions or not" (emphasis added). In Exodus 20, after the spectacular theophany of God on the top of Mt. Sinai and the declaration of the Ten Commandments by the voice of God, the Israelites trembled in fear. The response of Moses is instructive: "Do not be afraid; for God has come *only to test you* and to put the fear of him upon you so that you do not sin" (Exodus 20:20; emphasis added). Then, in Deuteronomy 8 Moses observes that the long sojourn in the wilderness has been purposeful: "Remember the long way that the LORD your God has led you these forty years in the wilderness, in order to humble you, *testing you to know what was in your heart*, whether or not you would keep his commandments" (Deuteronomy 8:2; emphasis added). Finally, the book of Job, while not using the language of testing, surely presents the tribulations of Job as a form of test to determine the true character of Job's devotion to God (Job 1-2). Testing in this sense is not about torturing someone with a situation of extreme distress; it is about ascertaining the true character of someone. Testing involves probing to expose one's character.

THE TESTING OF JESUS

In the case of Jesus, the devil through a series of three scenarios tests the character of Jesus and his commitment to God's way of mission. Having received the divine affirmation of his divine

Sonship, Jesus now is exposed to the extremities of choice. He might be God's Son through his extraordinary birth and by the proclamation of the voice from heaven but is Jesus really the Son of God where it counts—in his obedience to the will of God? Or is Jesus a fraudulent Son of God? One who chooses the shortcut and obedience to the devil in order to obtain what is his as the Son of God?

It also seems to me that if the proposals put to Jesus by the devil are a real test, then the outcome of this confrontation is not a foregone conclusion. For the test to be real there had to be at least the possibility that Jesus would choose the way of the devil. There is real jeopardy in this narrative. The fact that Jesus resisted the proposals of the devil and chose the way of obedience to his heavenly Father is critical to the story of Jesus and the accomplishment of his mission. Jesus's passing of this test is real as well. His obedience is a real decision made in a context in which a different decision *could have been made*.

Through the testing of Jesus, all involved come to know the true character of Jesus's divine Sonship. He is God's Son not only through his birth as a matter of status, but also through his life— this is confirmed by his obedience to the Father. It is in this light that the writer of the book of Hebrews can say of Jesus that he "in every respect has been tested as we are, yet without sin..." (Hebrews 4:15).

The departure of the devil from Jesus at the end of this trial in the wilderness does not mean that Jesus experienced no more tests throughout his life. The devil, referred to by a variety of names, makes a series of appearances throughout Matthew (for example, see 5:37; 6:13; 12:24,26, 27; 13:19, 38, 39; 16:23; 25:41). One of the most difficult tests for Jesus would come immediately after Peter's great declaration of Jesus's messiahship. For Peter this insight meant that Jesus would be the deliverer of Israel from subservience to its Roman oppressors and the re-establishment of the rule of David's dynasty. On this basis, Peter objected vehemently to Jesus's prediction of his suffering and death. But Jesus rejected Peter's objection, condemning Peter as the agent of Satan—testing his obedience to the path set before him by his heavenly Father (Matthew 16:13-23). Finally, in the Garden of Gethsemane, Jesus wrestled with his obedience to the will of his Father. He would have preferred to have avoided the cruel death he would experience; but Jesus clearly accepted obedience to his Father's will rather than exercising his own will (Matthew 26:36-39). The testing of Jesus is a frequent motif in Matthew. We must neither shy away from it nor water down the severity of the tests.

PASSING THE TEST

When the series of tests in Matthew 4 came to an end the devil withdrew from the scene and angels came to minister to Jesus. Jesus had shown himself to be the Son of God not simply because of his genealogy, his unique conception and birth, the appearance of a star in the night sky, the repeated fulfilment of prophetic proclamations, or the voice of God at his baptism, but also through the strength of his obedience to God his Father. He was the Son of God not because of his status but rather through his willingness to serve God. For Jesus divine sonship meant service and obedience. To paraphrase the voice from heaven at the end of the test of Abraham in Genesis 22, we might imagine God saying to Jesus, "*Now* I know that you truly are my Son!"

Chapter 23: The Wilderness

Matthew 4:1-11

John the Baptist appeared in the wilderness of Judaea (Matthew 3:1).   After his baptism, Jesus was led by the Spirit into the wilderness (Matthew 4:1).   Later in Matthew's gospel a vast crowd of more than 4,000 followed Jesus into the wilderness (Matthew 15:29-39) and after three days of instruction were fed with seven loaves and a small fish.   These three texts from Matthew are part of a collection of biblical references to important events that took place in the wilderness. What's the significance of the fact that these three stories take place in the wilderness? What is it about the wilderness that makes it so important in the biblical tradition?

The most fundamental characteristic of the wilderness is that it lacks water.   The scarcity of water makes the wilderness a dry place, a place in which there is a shortage of the basic resources to sustain life: water and food.   The Israelites experienced this scarcity shortly after they left Egypt at the time of the exodus. With the crossing of the Red Sea, the Israelite throng immediately was confronted by the shortage of water and food. For this reason the first stories in the book of Exodus after their departure from Egypt are dominated by concerns for the provision of food and water in a wilderness with few resources (see Exodus 15:22–17:7). In Matthew, this scarcity of resources in the wilderness is reflected in the sparse diet of John the Baptist (Matthew 3:4), in the 40-day fast of Jesus (Matthew 4:2), and in the dearth of food for the crowd (Matthew 15:32–33).

A PLACE OF DIVINE PROVISION

One of the interesting features of the wilderness motif is that it often stands in contrast to the abundance of more fertile land. The scarcity of food and water during their lengthy sojourn in the wilderness forced the Israelites to depend upon God for food and water. Their need was immediate; their reliance upon God for survival was undeniable. The dependence upon "daily bread" in the form of manna beginning in Exodus 16 came to signify the provision of God in a desolate land. But in the book of Deuteronomy, as Israel stood on the edge of the Promised Land, Moses warned them against the complacency and self-sufficiency that would test them once they experienced the abundance of the Promised Land. In contrast to the dearth of food in the wilderness, the relative affluence of life in Canaan would distract the Israelites from their immediate reliance upon God; it would anesthetize them to the need to seek the LORD. Abundance was a threat to Israel's focused reliance upon God for its survival. As interpreted in the book of Deuteronomy, the wilderness was a place where the Israelites should have had clarity about their reliance upon God and the relative affluence of life in the Promised Land could entice them to forget this.

A PLACE OF CLOSENESS TO GOD

Some remembered Israel's lengthy sojourn in the wilderness as a time when Israel was devoted to the LORD. The prophet Jeremiah compared this wilderness experience to the honeymoon of a newly married couple. Speaking in the voice of the LORD, Jeremiah observed, "I remember the devotion of your youth, your love as a bride, how you followed me in the wilderness, in a land not sown" (Jeremiah 2:2). Yet in the subsequent verses, God is stunned by Israel's turning away in its quest to find other "lovers." Apparently, life in the wilderness can be complicated.

Judaism had a history of groups withdrawing from the contaminations of city-life to seek the simplicity of life in the wilderness. For example, the Essenes who produced the Dead Sea Scrolls withdrew to the wilderness to live lives devoted to the service of God. For them, the wilderness became a place of communion with God; distractions were removed and the human heart was more receptive to God.

In the history of the Church, there have been many such as the so-called "desert fathers," who intentionally have sought the wilderness in their quest to draw closer to God. The distractions of everyday life are left behind; the complications of human interactions are stripped away in the pursuit of a single-minded encounter with God.

Perhaps it was the ability of the wilderness to draw attention away from abundance that led John the Baptist to his life and preaching in the wilderness. By separating himself and the crowds from the distractions of life in the cities and more cultivated land, John was making the crowds more receptive to his preaching. A journey from the city or farmable land into the wilderness was a way of stripping away the trappings of everyday life in order to come to clarity. It was a way of washing off the accumulated dust of the mundane and to see life through a different lens.

A PLACE OF TESTING

Yet this wilderness experience invariably leads to the recognition that the wilderness also is a place in which testing becomes more severe. The deprivations of the wilderness may remove us from many distractions and lay us open to the Spirit of God; but they may also lay bare the deep-seated temptations that we never knew were there. The wilderness, thus, often is a two-edged sword: removing distractions to open a path to God, but at the same time exposing us to the taunts of the devil.

In Israelite tradition the wilderness sojourn was remembered as a time of God's provision. The wilderness also was a place of testing: Israel was tempted to worship other gods, to complain about the provision of God (Numbers 11) and to rebel against the LORD. Israel's loyalty to the LORD was tested severely in the wilderness. And the journey through the wilderness also was a time of repeated acts of rebellion against God.

It is with this in the background that according to Matthew the Spirit of God led Jesus into the wilderness. To what end? It seems as though on the one hand the deprivations of the wilderness—exemplified in the 40-day fast—may have drawn Jesus closer to God; but on the other hand, they also exposed him to testing by the devil.

Jesus did not seek out this testing; he was led into the wilderness by the Spirit of God. There is no need for us to put ourselves in the place of testing; the test will come to us in its own time. Our time in the wilderness will come, the devil will test us, and the Spirit of God will be with us. We can be assured of this.

Chapter 24: Even the Devil Can Cite Scripture!

Matthew 4:1-11

What surprises me most about the story of the testing of Jesus by the devil is not the fact that the devil sets three tests in front of Jesus. Neither does it surprise me that the devil's tests have the potential to distract Jesus from his mission. Finally, it doesn't surprise me that Jesus responds to each test by quoting a text from the Old Testament. What really surprises me is that in the second test the devil is so proficient at quoting Scripture (Matthew 4:6). Apparently the Word of God can be wielded like a sword by the devil himself!

PROOF-TEXTS ARE THE DEVIL'S SWORD

When I read the story of the testing of Jesus, I am reminded of my Grade 9 English class in which our teacher guided our class through Shakespeare's play *The Merchant of Venice*. At a critical point in the play, one of Shakespeare's characters says, "The devil can cite Scripture for his purpose." As I have reflected on this statement in the intervening years, I have concluded that Shakespeare actually got it right. The devil—or any one of us—can indeed cite Scripture to serve just about any purpose and to support just about any position.

That's the problem with the Bible. Disputes over difficult theological and ethical issues are often fought by competing sides firing volleys of proof-texts at one another, trying to score cheap points and give their pet positions the appearance of scriptural authority. In Matthew 4:1-11 even the devil tested Jesus by quoting from Psalm 91. Think about that—the devil used Scripture to entice Jesus to disobey God! For his part, Jesus quoted a different verse back to the devil. For a brief moment Jesus's testing in the wilderness became a battle of biblical proof-texts.

The same battle of proof-texts continues to this day. Some time ago a prominent American politician cited Romans 13 and Paul's injunction to obey the laws of the Roman government to support the detention of refugees who enter the United States illegally, as well as the separation of children from their parents while in detention. On the other side of the controversy, there were those who cited the Old Testament prophets' injunctions to care for the widow, orphan and alien (that is, the non-citizen who lived in Israel) to argue that such treatment of refugees is immoral and unchristian. How is one to decide such a complex issue when different biblical passages can be deployed to support competing positions?

The problem is not limited to this one issue. In fact, we can find verses in the Bible to support almost any viewpoint on most contentious issues. On matters of economics, legal issues, and sexuality, it is possible to cite biblical passages that seem to contradict one another and support incompatible perspectives. I can even find a verse in some translations of the Book of Job that supports my distaste for eggs!

So if Scripture is so easily deployed to support almost any viewpoint—and even the purposes of the devil—how can we even begin to use the Bible to discern a Christian way forward? Or to assist our discernment on matters of Christian faith and practice? I have several suggestions.

SCRIPTURE CORRECTS US MORE THAN IT CONFIRMS OUR VIEWS

First, finding a verse in the Bible to support a particular position, viewpoint or action is not sufficient justification for that position, viewpoint or action. In fact, because I believe that the Bible is God's Word and not my word, my general stance is that finding a random verse or passage to support an opinion I already hold likely means that I am dictating the meaning of Scripture rather than allowing Scripture to speak its own word to me. The Bible is not a tool to support our viewpoints, but rather a means through which God shapes and corrects us. I should expect that Scripture will challenge me rather than confirm my viewpoint.

That's the point of the statement we read in 2 Timothy 3:16-17: "All Scripture is inspired by God and is useful for teaching, for reproof, for correction, and for training in righteousness, so that everyone who belongs to God may be proficient, equipped for every good work." The purpose of Scripture in its entirety and in its smallest passages is the cultivation of our Christian faith. Scripture—rightly interpreted—informs us, corrects us, and trains us in the ways of God in the world. The goal of reading Scripture is to prepare and equip us for service of God and our neighbour, not to support our particular viewpoint.

HEED SCRIPTURE'S OVERALL MESSAGE

Second, because even the devil can cite Scripture for his own purpose, we have to move beyond citing individual proof-texts from the Bible. That doesn't mean that we can ignore what the texts of the Bible say. But we can find helpful guidance from John Wesley the eighteenth-century English priest who led the great Methodist revival. Over his lifetime, Wesley argued that any individual passage in the Bible should be interpreted within the context of what he called "the general tenor of Scripture." What this means is that it is not individual proof-texts that have real authority; it is rather the general message, tone, instruction and purpose of Scripture that should guide our interpretation of individual passages. The meaning of individual passages is shaped by the overall message of Scripture, and an interpretation of any passage is compelling to the extent that it is consistent with that message.

SCRIPTURE STIRS LOVE FOR GOD AND LOVE FOR OUR NEIGHBOUR

Third, for Wesley the purpose of Scripture is to stir Christians toward greater love for God and greater love for our neighbour. Think about that for a moment. Perhaps that's a standard of interpretation that will help us. When interpreting a biblical text we should ask ourselves, How does our interpretation and application of our favourite proof-text or passage of Scripture, whatever it is, cultivate in us greater love for God and greater love for our neighbour? If it doesn't, then we need to reconsider our interpretation and entertain the possibility that we are hearing our own word rather than the Word of God.

READING SCRIPTURE SHOULD BE GUIDED BY THE SPIRIT

Finally, the interpretation of Scripture must always be done under the guidance and direction of the Holy Spirit. As Christians, we affirm that God not only inspired the Bible as it was written, but also that God continues to inspire the Scriptures as we read and interpret them. If we are to hear the words of Scripture as the Word of God, then we must do our best to ensure that our ears and hearts are attuned to the Holy Spirit. This requires that we be shaped and formed in our faith by the Spirit. The words on the page are lifeless until God breathes life into them as we receive them. Good people read the Bible well when they are guided by the Holy Spirit.

In the wilderness, Jesus was not alone with the devil. The Spirit of God had led him into the wilderness and remained there with him. His interpretation of Scripture was guided by the Spirit and ours must be as well. Thus Jesus was able to see that the devil's citation from Psalm 91 did not cultivate in him greater love for God or greater love for his neighbour. The devil's citation of Scripture, if accepted by Jesus, would have cultivated only Jesus's love for himself. It would have been self-serving. Jesus was able to see through this and in his own citation of Scripture used it to cultivate his love for God. That's the only way to avoid making the Bible a tool of the devil.

Guided by the Spirit of God, our interpretation of Scripture—whether of an individual verse or an entire book of the Bible—should move us away from inordinate love of ourselves and toward greater love of God and greater love of our neighbour.

Chapter 25: What Does the Testing of Jesus Teach Us?

Matthew 4:1-11

S tepping back from the details of the story about the devil testing Jesus in the wilderness we now must ask why this story matters. How should we understand it? Generally speaking, scholars have suggested three different ways to interpret the narrative in Matthew 4:1-11.

TWO CONTRASTING WILDERNESS EXPERIENCES

First of all, there are those who interpret the 40-day fast of Jesus in the wilderness and his testing by the devil as a parallel to the 40-year long testing of Israel in the wilderness after the Hebrew slaves had been liberated from Egyptian tyranny. As we have seen in a previous study, one of the purposes of the sojourn in the wilderness was to test Israel's devotion to God. In the wilderness, with its scarcity of food and water, the Israelites were forced to rely upon God's provision. But even in such extreme circumstances—perhaps even *because* of such extreme circumstances—the Israelites were tempted to seek out other sources of food and water. They grumbled, they rebelled, and on occasion sought out other gods to supply their needs. Sometimes they passed the test set before them; but many times the Israelites failed miserably.

By enduring a similar period of testing in the wilderness, Jesus provided a positive example of one who remained faithful in a period of testing. Where Israel had failed, Jesus succeeded. Jesus overcame the tests set before him in a way that contrasted with Israel's frequent failures. According to Matthew, Jesus's successful passing of the series of three tests marked the beginning of the new community of the faithful that Jesus came to establish. The ministry of Jesus, as important as it was for its own sake, was understood by Matthew to be the beginning of the new community of those who would follow Jesus. In a sense, the obedience and faithfulness of Jesus in the wilderness launched this new community. It was the beginning of a new moment in salvation-history.

The Gospel of Matthew is deeply concerned about the character of this new community. The Sermon on the Mount (Matthew 5–7) describes in detail the "greater righteousness" that should characterize the people of God that Jesus is calling into existence. But it all begins with the obedience of Jesus in the wilderness. Without that, the rest of Matthew would not make sense.

WHAT KIND OF MESSIAH?

The second interpretation of the testing of Jesus in the wilderness also takes into account the larger story that Matthew narrates. In this interpretation the tests set before Jesus by the devil are focused on the character of the messiahship that Jesus will embody. Will Jesus's messiahship be focused on glory, on razzle dazzle, or on spectacular displays of divine power? Will his messiahship be seen in the overthrow of the Roman oppressors and its replacement with a new Jewish autonomy? Will Jesus be a new King David, sitting upon a throne and attended by humble servants? Will those closest to Jesus share in that power and that glory? That, after all, appears to have been the expectation of Peter and the other disciples when Peter confessed Jesus's messiahship in Matthew 16:16. But in the wilderness we see Jesus reject such a messiahship—not because he personally found it distasteful but rather because it represented a human and devilish agenda rather than the will of God. Jesus chose the way of obedience rather than the way of self-determination and autonomy. He chose obedience to his Father over the shortcut to glory promised to him by the devil. And while the testing in the wilderness set the tone for Jesus's life and ministry, his departure from the wilderness did not mean that this temptation to power and glory had passed. Later in Matthew we find that Jesus faced similar tests: in Peter's expectation that Jesus's messiahship excluded suffering; in the agonizing prayer in Gethsemane about what path to follow (Matthew 26:36-46); and in the drawn-sword response of some of the disciples to Jesus's arrest (Matthew 26:51-56) Jesus had to make the decision about the quality of his messiahship.

According to this interpretation of the testing of Jesus, nothing less than the mission of Jesus was at stake in the wilderness. Jesus chose the mission of service, humility and obedience to his Father over the false mission of power, lording it over others and self-assertion. According to Matthew, the decision of Jesus should be definitive for the Church. To be the Church—the new community established by Jesus—the followers of Jesus must follow his path, accept his definition of mission. The mission of the Church is not to be defined by power, glory, money and influence; it is to be defined by obedience to God, humility, faithfulness, and service. The testing of Jesus in the wilderness set this tone for us.

A MODEL TO FOLLOW

Finally, the third interpretation of the testing of Jesus in the wilderness emphasizes the tests that Jesus faced as typical of the tests that all Christians face. According to this interpretation, Jesus is a model for how we both are tested to choose autonomy over obedience and how we are to respond to those tests. Jesus was subject to all the various tests that confront the rest of us as humans. He shares with us the experience of temptation. But he provides the model of how we are able to resist the wiles of the devil. If we follow Jesus we shall be able to obey. We shall be able to be true followers of Jesus.

The key element of Jesus's resistance to the tests to which he was subjected was his reliance upon the Scriptures. Especially important in the responses of Jesus to the devil was the book of Deuteronomy. This should not be surprising because the focus of Deuteronomy is on the two issues that would dominate Matthew: the call to uncompromising obedience to God and the nature of the community that God was calling into existence. From beginning to end, Deuteronomy calls Israel to undivided loyalty to the LORD. But it also calls Israel to be a community that stands in stark contrast to the nations around it. Israel is to be a community of brothers and sisters who care for one another and who serve one another. It is to be a community in which power, resources, and influence are shared broadly. If we read Matthew carefully, we find that these same qualities are to be embodied within the new community that Jesus is establishing. With one exception: the followers of Jesus are to practice an even greater righteousness!

The temptation to follow a different path is in front of us continuously. But if we read Matthew closely—beginning with the testing of Jesus in the wilderness—we will see that Jesus models for us the path of righteousness. It seems to me that each of these three interpretations teaches us something important about our identity and mission as the Church. It clarifies the tests that are set before us; but it also clarifies the path to passing those tests successfully.

Chapter 26: The Light Has Come

Matthew 4:12-17

Matthew marked a major transition in the story of Jesus with the notation that John the Baptist had been arrested. No details of John's arrest are provided; they are not relevant to Matthew's main storyline. But the arrest of John prompted Jesus to leave the Judean wilderness for the relative obscurity and safety of Galilee.

GALILEE OF THE GENTILES

Galilee was considered to be a backwater by many Jews from the south. It had a murky reputation. But for Matthew, Galilee was important for four reasons. First, it was presented as the place where Jesus's public ministry began and where much of it was conducted. Second, after the resurrection it was in Galilee that Jesus appeared to his disciples (Matthew 28:10). Third, it was in Galilee that Jesus delivered his commission to his closest followers to make disciples of all nations (Matthew 28:16-20) in his final address to them. It was from Galilee that Jesus launched the mission of the Church and inaugurated the new Christian community embracing all nations. Finally, and perhaps most importantly for Matthew, he was able to identify a prophetic text from Isaiah 9:1-2 that speaks of "Galilee of the Gentiles." Some scholars have suggested that Matthew's use of a citation from Isaiah here fends off the embarrassment of Jesus's association with Galilee. After all, nothing good—and certainly not the Messiah—can come from Galilee (John 7:40-52). But even more important than defending Jesus against suspicions aroused by his Galilean origin is the fact that Matthew's citation of these verses follows his pattern of anchoring the events of Jesus's birth, appearance and mission in the words of Old Testament prophets, thereby confirming these events as part of the divine plan. For Matthew, while Galilee may have been a backwater and the brunt of Judean prejudices, it is the place of Jesus's upbringing, the commencement of his ministry as well as much of his public ministry, and the culminating commission to make disciples of all nations.

FROM DARKNESS TO LIGHT

The citation from Isaiah 9:1-2 has an additional purpose. As Matthew cites these verses they read in part, "the people who sat in darkness have seen a great light, and for those who sat in the region and shadow of death light has dawned." In biblical imagery, darkness is associated with evil, misfortune, and even death. Beginning with the creation story in Genesis 1 and the description of darkness covering the face of the deep, darkness is seen as opposed to God or to the creative, salvific purposes of God. In contrast, light represents what is good and productive. Light even becomes an image for salvation. The beginning of Jesus's public ministry, therefore, marks the transition from darkness to light, from peril to salvation. The darkness of sin is being overcome by the light of salvation that comes through Jesus.

THE TURNING POINT

Finally, in words that match exactly the proclamation of John the Baptist in Matthew 3:2, Jesus begins his public ministry with a summons to repentance because the kingdom of heaven has come near. As noted earlier, the call to repentance is a summons to radical change and transformation. As the kingdom draws near the old must be put aside and the new life must be embraced. According to Matthew, the arrival of Jesus marks the critical turning-point. Everything has changed.

DECISION TIME

From Matthew's perspective, those who hear the news of the kingdom's arrival are forced to make a decision about their response to this news. Again and again throughout Matthew, people are called to embrace the kingdom of heaven. They are called to embrace Jesus as the messianic bringer of the kingdom.

But the summons of Jesus to repentance because of the arrival of the kingdom of heaven is not limited to those who first heard his words or to the first readers of Matthew's Gospel. It is a summons that continues to be proclaimed wherever Matthew is read. No less than in the case of that first audience or in the case of Matthew's own Christian community, we too are called to repentance—to a radical reorientation and transformation in the light of the kingdom of heaven that came with Jesus the Christ—son of Abraham, son of David, and Son of God.

Further Reading

For ease of reading, I have chosen not to include references for the specific sources of information I have used in these reflections. I have benefitted immensely from the labours of countless scholars and commentators. I am grateful to them for their diligence and insights. I want to acknowledge their contributions to my own thinking.

* * *

There is an almost limitless wealth of resources available to assist our reading and interpretation of Matthew. Out of the bookshelf of resources that I have found most beneficial to my personal study of Matthew, I want to make a few suggestions about books that could be helpful for additional study of this Gospel.

Collins, Kenneth J., and Robert W. Wall, eds. *Wesley One Volume Commentary on the Bible.* Nashville: Abingdon, 2020.

This new one volume commentary on the Bible provides a good overview of Matthew with special attention to the ways in which Matthew's story of Jesus connects with the theology of John Wesley. The volume will be useful for the study of any biblical book.

Nativity

* * *

Long, Thomas G. *Matthew*. Westminster Bible Companion. Louisville: Westminster John Knox Press, 1997.
This is a good, relatively brief (348 pages) commentary on Matthew. Long provides an introduction to Matthew and then proceeds to comment on the text paragraph by paragraph. There are good insights throughout the commentary.

Kingsbury, Jack Dean. *Matthew as Story*. 2nd ed. Minneapolis: Fortress Press, 1988.
This is one of my all-time favourite books about Matthew's Gospel. Kingsbury has had a major influence on the interpretation of Matthew and this book provides a sound overview of how Matthew tells his story of Jesus.

* * *

Nolland, John. *The Gospel of Matthew: A Commentary on the Greek Text*. New International Greek Testament Commentary. Grand Rapids: Eerdmans, 2005.

France, Richard Thomas. *The Gospel According to Matthew: An Introduction and Commentary*. New International Commentary on the New Testament. Grand Rapids: Eerdmans, 2007.

Keener, Craig S. *The Gospel of Matthew: A Socio-Rhetorical Commentary*. Grand Rapids: Eerdmans, 2009.

These three commentaries are each major works on Matthew. They are very detailed and challenging. They would be useful for an advanced study of Matthew.

* * *

Brown, Jeannine K., and Kyle Roberts. *Matthew*. The Two Horizons New Testament Commentary. Grand Rapids: Eerdmans, 2018.

This recent commentary interprets Matthew theologically. It includes a section-by-section discussion of Matthew, but then moves to a more theological consideration of various themes in Matthew.

About the Author

Don Burke is Professor of Biblical Studies at Booth University College in Winnipeg, Canada where he has taught for many years. In 2018 and 2019 he won awards from the Canadian Church Press for the best Biblical Interpretation in a Canadian church publication (*Salvationist*). He brings his experience as a professor and writer to this book to invite others to draw closer to God in their Christian understanding and experience.

Made in the USA
Columbia, SC
13 November 2020